HBR'S 10 MUST READS

On
Managing
People
(Vol. 2)

HBR's 10 Must Reads series is the definitive collection of ideas and best practices for aspiring and experienced leaders alike. These books offer essential reading selected from the pages of *Harvard Business Review* on topics critical to the success of every manager.

Titles include:

HBR's 10 Must Reads 2015
HBR's 10 Must Reads 2016
HBR's 10 Must Reads 2017
HBR's 10 Must Reads 2018
HBR's 10 Must Reads 2019
HBR's 10 Must Reads 2020
HBR's 10 Must Reads for CEOs
HBR's 10 Must Reads for New Managers
HBR's 10 Must Reads on AI, Analytics, and the New Machine Age
HBR's 10 Must Reads on Boards
HBR's 10 Must Reads on Building a Great Culture
HBR's 10 Must Reads on Business Model Innovation
HBR's 10 Must Reads on Change Management
HBR's 10 Must Reads on Collaboration
HBR's 10 Must Reads on Communication
HBR's 10 Must Reads on Design Thinking
HBR's 10 Must Reads on Diversity
HBR's 10 Must Reads on Emotional Intelligence
HBR's 10 Must Reads on Entrepreneurship and Startups
HBR's 10 Must Reads on Innovation
HBR's 10 Must Reads on Leadership
HBR's 10 Must Reads on Leadership (Vol. 2)
HBR's 10 Must Reads on Leadership for Healthcare
HBR's 10 Must Reads on Leadership Lessons from Sports
HBR's 10 Must Reads on Making Smart Decisions
HBR's 10 Must Reads on Managing Across Cultures
HBR's 10 Must Reads on Managing in a Downturn
HBR's 10 Must Reads on Managing People
HBR's 10 Must Reads on Managing People (Vol. 2)

On
Managing
People
(Vol. 2)

HARVARD BUSINESS REVIEW PRESS
Boston, Massachusetts

Library of Congress Cataloging-in-Publication Data

Title: HBR's 10 must reads on managing people. Vol. 2.
Other titles: On managing people. Vol. 2. | HBR's 10 must reads (Series)
Description: Boston : Harvard Business Review Press, [2020] | Series: HBR's 10 must reads
Identifiers: LCCN 2019041069 (print) | LCCN 2019041070 (ebook) | ISBN 9781633699137 (paperback) | ISBN 9781633699144 (ebook)
Subjects: LCSH: Supervision of employees. | Management. | Personnel management.
Classification: LCC HF5549.12 .H395 2020 (print) | LCC HF5549.12 (ebook) | DDC 658.3—dc23
LC record available at https://lccn.loc.gov/2019041069
LC ebook record available at https://lccn.loc.gov/2019041070

ISBN: 978-1-63369-913-7
eISBN: 978-1-63369-914-4

Contents

On
Managing
People
(Vol. 2)

Are You a Good Boss— or a Great One?

by Linda A. Hill and Kent Lineback

"AM I GOOD ENOUGH?"

"Am I ready? This is my big opportunity, but now I'm not sure I'm prepared."

These thoughts plagued Jason, an experienced manager, as he lay awake one night fretting about a new position he'd taken. For more than five years he had run a small team of developers in Boston. They produced two highly successful lines of engineering textbooks for the education publishing arm of a major media conglomerate. On the strength of his reputation as a great manager of product development, he'd been chosen by the company to take over an online technical-education startup based in London.

Jason arrived at his new office on a Monday morning, excited and confident, but by the end of his first week he was beginning to wonder whether he was up to the challenge. In his previous work he had led people who'd worked together before and required coordination but little supervision. There were problems, of course, but nothing like what he'd discovered in this new venture. Key members of his group barely talked to one another. Other publishers in the company, whose materials and collaboration he desperately needed, angrily viewed his new group as competition. The goals he'd been set seemed impossible—the group was about to miss some early milestones—and a crucial partnership with an outside organization had been badly, perhaps irretrievably, damaged. On top of all that, his boss, who was located in New York, offered little help. "That's why you're there" was the typical response whenever Jason described a problem. By Friday he was worried about living up to the expectations implied in that response.

Do Jason's feelings sound familiar? Such moments of doubt and even fear may and often do come despite years of management experience. Any number of events can trigger them: An initiative you're running isn't going as expected. Your people aren't performing as they should. You hear talk in the group that "the real problem here is lack of leadership." You think you're doing fine until you, like Jason, receive a daunting new assignment. You're given a lukewarm performance review. Or one day you simply realize that you're no longer growing and advancing—you're stuck.

Most Managers Stop Working on Themselves

The whole question of how managers grow and advance is one we've studied, thought about, and lived with for years. As a professor working with high potentials, MBAs, and executives from around the globe, Linda meets people who want to contribute to their organizations and build fulfilling careers. As an executive, Kent has worked with managers at all levels of both private and public organizations. All our experience brings us to a simple but troubling observation: Most bosses reach a certain level of proficiency and stop there—short of what they could and should be.

We've discussed this observation with countless colleagues, who almost without exception have seen what we see: Organizations usually have a few great managers, some capable ones, a horde of mediocre ones, some poor ones, and some awful ones. The great majority of people we work with are well-intentioned, smart, accomplished individuals. Many progress and fulfill their ambitions. But too many derail and fail to live up to their potential. Why? Because they stop working on themselves.

Managers rarely ask themselves, "How good am I?" and "Do I need to be better?" unless they're shocked into it. When did *you*

Idea in Brief

Many managers underestimate the transformational challenges of their roles—or they become complacent and stop growing and improving. At best they learn to get by; at worst they become terrible bosses. Sometimes even the best of them suffer doubts and fears despite years of management experience.

Three imperatives can guide managers on their journey to becoming great bosses: (1) *Manage yourself*. Productive influence comes from people's trust in your competence and character. (2) *Manage your network*. The organization as a whole must be engaged to create the conditions for your own and your team's success. (3) *Manage your team*. Effective managers forge a high-performing "we" out of all the individuals who report to them.

Constant and probing self-assessment across these three imperatives is essential, the authors write. They include a useful assessment tool to help readers get started.

last ask those questions? On the spectrum of great to awful bosses, where do you fall?

Managers in new assignments usually start out receptive to change. The more talented and ambitious ones choose stretch assignments, knowing that they'll have much to learn at first. But as they settle in and lose their fear of imminent failure, they often grow complacent. Every organization has its ways of doing things— policies, standard practices, and unspoken guidelines, such as "promote by seniority" and "avoid conflict." Once they're learned, managers often use them to get by—to "manage" in the worst sense of the word.

It doesn't help that a majority of the organizations we see offer their managers minimal support and rarely press the experienced ones to improve. Few expect more of their leaders than short-term results, which by themselves don't necessarily indicate real management skill.

In our experience, however, the real culprit is neither managerial complacency nor organizational failure: It is a lack of understanding. When bosses are questioned, it's clear that many of them have stopped making progress because they simply *don't know how to.*

Do you understand what's required to become truly effective?
Too often managers underestimate how much time and effort it takes to keep growing and developing. Becoming a great boss is a lengthy, difficult process of learning and change, driven mostly by personal experience. Indeed, so much time and effort are required that you can think of the process as a journey—a journey of years.

What makes the journey especially arduous is that the lessons involved cannot be taught. Leadership is using yourself as an instrument to get things done in the organization, so it is about self-development. There are no secrets and few shortcuts. You and every other manager must learn the lessons yourself, based on your own experience as a boss. If you don't understand the nature of the journey, you're more likely to pause or lose hope and tell yourself, "I can't do this" or "I'm good enough already."

Do you understand what you're trying to attain?
We all know how disorganized, fragmented, and even chaotic every manager's workdays are. Given this reality, which is intensifying as work and organizations become more complex and fluid, how can you as a boss do anything more than cope with what comes at you day by day?

To deal with the chaos, you need a clear underlying sense of what's important and where you and your group want to be in the future. You need a mental model that you can lay over the chaos and into which you can fit all the messy pieces as they come at you. This way of thinking begins with a straightforward definition: Management is responsibility for the performance of a group of people.

It's a simple idea, yet putting it into practice is difficult, because management is *defined* by responsibility but *done* by exerting influence. To influence others you must make a difference not only in what they do but also in the thoughts and feelings that drive their actions. How do you actually do this?

To answer that question, you need an overarching, integrated way of thinking about your work as a manager. We offer an approach based on studies of management practice, our own observations, and our knowledge of where managers tend to go wrong. We call it the *three imperatives*: Manage yourself. Manage your network. Manage your team.

Is this the only way to describe management? No, of course not. But it's clear, straightforward, and, above all, focused on what managers must actually do. People typically think of "management" as just the third imperative, but today all three are critical to success. Together they encompass the crucial activities that effective managers must perform to influence others. Mastering them is the purpose of your journey.

Manage Yourself

Management begins with you, because who you are as a person, what you think and feel, the beliefs and values that drive your actions, and especially how you connect with others all matter to the people you must influence. Every day those people examine every interaction with you, your every word and deed, to uncover your intentions. They ask themselves, "Can I trust this person?" How hard they work, their level of personal commitment, their willingness to accept your influence, will depend in large part on the qualities they see in you. And their perceptions will determine the answer to this fundamental question every manager must ask: Am I someone who can influence others productively?

Who you are shows up most clearly in the relationships you form with others, especially those for whom you're responsible. It's easy to get those crucial relationships wrong. Effective managers possess the self-awareness and self-management required to get them right.

José, a department head, told us of two managers who worked for him in the marketing department of a large maker of durable goods. Both managers were struggling to deliver the results expected of their groups. Both, it turned out, were creating dysfunctional relationships. One was frankly ambivalent about being "the boss" and hated it when people referred to him that way. He wanted to be liked, so he tried to build close personal relationships. He would say, in effect, "Do what I ask because we're friends." That worked for a while until, for good reasons, he had to turn down one "friend" for

5

promotion and deny another one a bonus. Naturally, those people felt betrayed, and their dissatisfaction began to poison the feelings of everyone else in the group.

The other manager took the opposite approach. With her it was all business. No small talk or reaching out to people as people. For her, results mattered, and she'd been made the boss because she was the one who knew what needed to be done; it was the job of her people to execute. Not surprisingly, her message was always "Do what I say because I'm the boss." She was effective—until people began leaving.

If productive influence doesn't arise from being liked ("I'm your friend!") or from fear ("I'm the boss!"), where does it come from? From people's trust in you as a manager. That trust has two components: belief in your *competence* (you know what to do and how to do it) and belief in your *character* (your motives are good and you want your people to do well).

Trust is the foundation of all forms of influence other than coercion, and you need to conduct yourself with others in ways that foster it. Management really does begin with who you are as a person.

Manage Your Network

We once talked to Kim, the head of a software company division, just as he was leaving a meeting of a task force consisting of his peers. He had proposed a new way of handling interdivisional sales, which he believed would increase revenue by encouraging each division to cross-sell other divisions' products. At the meeting he'd made an extremely well-researched, carefully reasoned, and even compelling case for his proposal—which the group rejected with very little discussion. "How many of these people did you talk to about your proposal before the meeting?" we asked. None, it turned out. "But I anticipated all their questions and objections," he protested, adding with some bitterness, "It's just politics. If they can't see what's good for the company and them, I can't help them."

Many managers resist the need to operate effectively in their organizations' political environments. They consider politics dysfunctional—a sign the organization is broken—and don't realize that it unavoidably arises from three features inherent in all organizations: *division of labor,* which creates disparate groups with disparate and even conflicting goals and priorities; *interdependence,* which means that none of those groups can do their work without the others; and *scarce resources,* for which groups necessarily compete. Obviously, some organizations handle the politics better than others, but conflict and competition among groups are inevitable. How do they get resolved? Through organizational influence. Groups whose managers have influence tend to get what they need; other groups don't.

Unfortunately, many managers deal with conflict by trying to avoid it. "I hate company politics!" they say. "Just let me do my job." But effective managers know they cannot turn away. Instead, with integrity and for good ends, they proactively engage the organization to create the conditions for their success. They build and nurture a broad network of ongoing relationships with those they need and those who need them; that is how they influence people over whom they have no formal authority. They also take responsibility for making their boss, a key member of their network, a source of influence on their behalf.

Manage Your Team

As a manager, Wei worked closely with each of her people, who were spread across the United States and the Far East. But she rarely called a virtual group meeting, and only once had her group met face-to-face. "In my experience," she told us, "meetings online or in person are usually a waste of time. Some people do all the yakking, others stay silent, and not much gets done. It's a lot more efficient for me to work with each person and arrange for them to coordinate when that's necessary." It turned out, though, that she was spending all her time "coordinating," which included a great deal of conflict mediation. People under her seemed to be constantly at odds, vying for the scarce resources they needed to achieve their disparate goals and complaining about what others were or were not doing.

Too many managers overlook the possibilities of creating a real team and managing their people as a whole. They don't realize that managing one-on-one is just not the same as managing a group and that they can influence individual behavior much more effectively through the group, because most of us are social creatures who want to fit in and be accepted as part of the team. How do you make the people who work for you, whether on a project or permanently, into a real team—a group of people who are mutually committed to a common purpose and the goals related to that purpose?

To do collective work that requires varied skills, experience, and knowledge, teams are more creative and productive than groups of individuals who merely cooperate. In a real team, members hold themselves and one another jointly accountable. They share a genuine conviction that they will succeed or fail together. A clear and compelling purpose, and concrete goals and plans based on that purpose, are critical. Without them no group will coalesce into a real team.

Team culture is equally important. Members need to know what's required of them collectively and individually; what the team's values, norms, and standards are; how members are expected to work together (what kind of conflict is acceptable or unacceptable, for example); and how they should communicate. It's your job to make sure they have all this crucial knowledge.

Effective managers also know that even in a cohesive team they cannot ignore individual members. Every person wants to be a valued member of a group *and* needs individual recognition. You must be able to provide the attention members need, but always in the context of the team.

And finally, effective managers know how to lead a team through the work it does day after day—including the unplanned problems and opportunities that frequently arise—to make progress toward achieving their own and the team's goals.

Be Clear on How You're Doing

The three imperatives will help you influence both those who work for you and those who don't. Most important, they provide a clear and actionable road map for your journey. You must master them to become a fully effective manager.

These imperatives are not simply distinct managerial competencies. They are tightly integrated activities, each of which depends on the others. Getting your person-to-person relationships right is critical to building a well-functioning team and giving its individual members the attention they need. A compelling team purpose, bolstered by clear goals and plans, is the foundation for a strong network, and a network is indispensable for reaching your team's goals.

Knowing where you're going is only the first half of what's required. You also need to know at all times where you are on your journey and what you must do to make progress. We're all aware that the higher you rise in an organization, the less feedback you get about your performance. You have to be prepared to regularly assess yourself.

Too many managers seem to assume that development happens automatically. They have only a vague sense of the goal and of where they stand in relation to it. They tell themselves, "I'm doing all right" or "As I take on more challenges, I'll get better." Consequently, those managers fall short. There's no substitute for routinely taking a look at yourself and how you're doing. (The exhibit "Measuring yourself on the three imperatives" will help you do this.)

Don't be discouraged if you find several areas in which you could do better. No manager will meet all the standards implicit in the three imperatives. The goal is not perfection. It's developing the strengths you need for success and compensating for any fatal shortcomings. Look at your strengths and weaknesses in the context of your organization. What knowledge and skills does it—or will it—need to reach its goals? How can your strengths help it move forward? Given its needs and priorities, what weaknesses must you address right away? The answers become your personal learning goals.

What You Can Do Right Now

Progress will come only from your work experience: from trying and learning, observing and interacting with others, experimenting, and sometimes pushing yourself beyond the bounds of comfort—and then assessing yourself on the three imperatives again and again.

Measuring yourself on the three imperatives

Are you performing all the activities necessary to be an effective boss?
To get some sense of where you stand, assess yourself on the following questions:

		I need to make progress				This is a strength
Manage yourself	1. Do you use your formal authority effectively?	This is a strength if you consider it a useful tool but not your primary means of influencing others. You make clear why you do what you do—and even share your authority with others when possible and appropriate. You focus more on the responsibilities that come with authority than on the personal privileges it provides.	1	2	3	4	5
	2. Do you create thoughtful but not overly personal relationships?	This is a strength if your relationships are rich in human connections but always focused on the purpose and goals of the team and the organization. You avoid trying to influence people by befriending them.	1	2	3	4	5
	3. Do others trust you as a manager?	This is a strength if people, particularly your own, believe in your competence, intentions, and values. You demonstrate concern for their individual success.	1	2	3	4	5
	4. Do you exercise your influence ethically?	This is a strength if you consistently identify stakeholders, weigh their interests, and try to mitigate any harm that your actions may cause as you attempt to accomplish a greater good.	1	2	3	4	5

Manage your network		1	2	3	4	5
5. Do you systematically identify those who should be in your network?	This is a strength if you are always aware of which people and groups you and your team depend on, and vice versa, as circumstances change.	1	2	3	4	5
6. Do you proactively build and maintain your network?	This is a strength if you create and sustain relationships with those in your network, connect frequently with them, and support their needs.	1	2	3	4	5
7. Do you use your network to provide the protection and resources your team needs?	This is a strength if you protect your team from distractions and misunderstandings, use your network to solve problems inside and outside the team, and secure the funds, people, and other resources it needs.	1	2	3	4	5
8. Do you use your network to accomplish your team's goals?	This is a strength if you form coalitions of network members to support your team's goals and help others in your network achieve theirs. Your network colleagues believe in your competence and character.	1	2	3	4	5

(continued)

Measuring yourself on the three imperatives (continued)

		I need to make progress				This is a strength
Manage your team	9. Do you define and constantly refine your team's vision for the future?	This is a strength if you've defined your team's purpose and the goals, strategies, and actions that will take you there. You constantly gather information, discuss your plans with others, and refine your ideas.	1	2	3	4	5
	10. Do you clarify roles, work rules, team culture, and feedback about performance for your team?	This is a strength if your people feel a strong sense of "we"—that they're all pulling together toward the same worthwhile goals. They know how they individually contribute and what the team's work involves. They receive regular feedback from you.	1	2	3	4	5
	11. Do you know and manage your people as individuals as well as team members?	This is a strength if you interact equitably with all team members individually. You delegate, strive to help people grow, and constantly assess their performance. You hire people who both fit the team and add diversity, and you deal with performance issues quickly.	1	2	3	4	5
	12. Do you use daily activities and problems to pursue the three imperatives?	This is a strength if you regularly consider how every problem, obligation, or event can help you build your team, make progress on its goals, develop people, and strengthen your network.	1	2	3	4	5

How did you do? Did your responses cover the whole range from 1 to 5? If you consistently assessed yourself at 3 or above, you should be skeptical. In our experience, few bosses merit high ratings across the board. Did you give yourself mostly 3s? Take care not to hide in the middle, telling yourself, "I'm OK—not great, but not failing either." And don't be satisfied to stay there. "I'm not failing" is the watchword of those who are comfortable—and stuck.

Above all, take responsibility for your own development; ultimately, all development is self-development.

You won't make progress unless you consciously act. Before you started a business, you would draw up a business plan broken into manageable steps with milestones; do the same as you think about your journey. Set personal goals. Solicit feedback from others. Take advantage of company training programs. Create a network of trusted advisers, including role models and mentors. Use your strengths to seek out developmental experiences. We know you've heard all this advice before, and it is good advice. But what we find most effective is building the learning into your daily work.

For this purpose we offer a simple approach we call *prep, do, review.*

Prep

Begin each morning with a quick preview of the coming day's events. For each one, ask yourself how you can use it to develop as a manager and in particular how you can work on your specific learning goals. Consider delegating a task you would normally take on yourself and think about how you might do that—to whom, what questions you should ask, what boundaries or limits you should set, what preliminary coaching you might provide. Apply the same thinking during the day when a problem comes up unexpectedly. Before taking any action, step back and consider how it might help you become better. Stretch yourself. If you don't move outside familiar patterns and practice new approaches, you're unlikely to learn.

Do

Take whatever action is required in your daily work, and as you do, use the new and different approaches you planned. Don't lose your resolve. For example, if you tend to cut off conflict in a meeting, even constructive conflict, force yourself to hold back so that disagreement can be expressed and worked through. Step in only if the discussion becomes personal or points of view are being stifled. The ideas that emerge may lead you to a better outcome.

Review

After the action, examine what you did and how it turned out. This is where learning actually occurs. Reflection is critical, and it works best if you make it a regular practice. For example, set aside time toward the end of each day—perhaps on your commute home. Which actions worked well? What might you have done differently? Replay conversations. Compare what you did with what you might have done if you were the manager you aspire to be. Where did you disappoint yourself, and how did that happen? Did you practice any new behaviors or otherwise make progress on your journey?

Some managers keep notes about how they spent their time, along with thoughts about what they learned. One CEO working on a corporate globalization strategy told us he'd started recording every Friday his reflections about the past week. Within six weeks, he said, he'd developed greater discipline to say no to anything "not on the critical path," which gave him time to spend with key regulators and to jump-start the strategy.

If you still need to make progress on your journey, that should spur you to action, not discourage you. You can become what you want and need to be. But you must take personal responsibility for mastering the three imperatives and assessing where you are now.

Originally published in January–February 2011. Reprint R1101K

Let Your Workers Rebel

by Francesca Gino

THROUGHOUT OUR CAREERS, we are taught to conform—to the status quo, to the opinions and behaviors of others, and to information that supports our views. The pressure only grows as we climb the organizational ladder. By the time we reach high-level positions, conformity has been so hammered into us that we perpetuate it in our enterprises. In a recent survey I conducted of more than 2,000 employees across a wide range of industries, nearly half the respondents reported working in organizations where they regularly feel the need to conform, and more than half said that people in their organizations do not question the status quo. The results were similar when I surveyed high-level executives and midlevel managers. As this data suggests, organizations consciously or unconsciously urge employees to check a good chunk of their real selves at the door. Workers and their organizations both pay a price: decreased engagement, productivity, and innovation (see the exhibit "The perils of conformity").

Drawing on my research and fieldwork and on the work of other scholars of psychology and management, I will describe three reasons for our conformity on the job, discuss why this behavior is costly for organizations, and suggest ways to combat it.

Of course, not all conformity is bad. But to be successful and evolve, organizations need to strike a balance between adherence to the formal and informal rules that provide necessary structure and the freedom that helps employees do their best work. The pendulum has swung too far in the direction of conformity. In another recent survey I conducted, involving more than 1,000 employees in a variety of industries, less than 10% said they worked in companies that regularly encourage nonconformity. That's not surprising: For decades the principles of scientific management have prevailed. Leaders have been overly focused on designing efficient processes and getting employees to follow them. Now they need to think about when conformity hurts their business and allow—even promote— what I call *constructive nonconformity*: behavior that deviates from organizational norms, others' actions, or common expectations, to the benefit of the organization.

Why Conformity Is So Prevalent

Let's look at the three main, and interrelated, reasons why we so often conform at work.

We fall prey to social pressure

Early in life we learn that tangible benefits arise from following social rules about what to say, how to act, how to dress, and so on. Conforming makes us feel accepted and part of the majority. As classic research conducted in the 1950s by the psychologist Solomon Asch showed, conformity to peer pressure is so powerful that it occurs even when we know it will lead us to make bad decisions. In one experiment, Asch asked participants to complete what they believed was a simple perceptual task: identifying which of three lines on one card was the same length as a line on another card. When asked individually, participants chose the correct line. When asked in the presence of paid actors who intentionally selected the wrong line, about 75% conformed to the group at least once. In other words, they chose an incorrect answer in order to fit in.

Organizations have long exploited this tendency. Ancient Roman families employed professional mourners at funerals. Entertainment companies hire people ("claques") to applaud at performances. And companies advertising health products often report the percentage of doctors or dentists who use their offerings.

Conformity at work takes many forms: modeling the behavior of others in similar roles, expressing appropriate emotions, wearing proper attire, routinely agreeing with the opinions of managers, acquiescing to a team's poor decisions, and so on. And all too often, bowing to peer pressure reduces individuals' engagement with their jobs. This is understandable: Conforming often conflicts with our true preferences and beliefs and therefore makes us feel inauthentic. In fact, research I conducted with Maryam Kouchaki, of Northwestern University, and Adam Galinsky, of Columbia University, showed that when people feel inauthentic at work, it's usually because they have succumbed to social pressure to conform.

We become too comfortable with the status quo

In organizations, standard practices—the usual ways of thinking and doing—play a critical role in shaping performance over time. But they can also get us stuck, decrease our engagement, and constrain our ability to innovate or to perform at a high level. Rather than resulting from thoughtful choices, many traditions endure out of routine, or what psychologists call the *status quo bias*. Because we feel validated and reassured when we stick to our usual ways of thinking and doing, and because—as research has consistently found—we weight the potential losses of deviating from the status quo much more heavily than we do the potential gains, we favor decisions that maintain the current state of affairs.

But sticking with the status quo can lead to boredom, which in turn can fuel complacency and stagnation. Borders, BlackBerry, Polaroid, and Myspace are but a few of the many companies that once had winning formulas but didn't update their strategies until it was too late. Overly comfortable with the status quo, their leaders fell back on tradition and avoided the type of nonconformist behavior that could have spurred continued success.

We interpret information in a self-serving manner

A third reason for the prevalence of conformity is that we tend to prioritize information that supports our existing beliefs and to ignore information that challenges them, so we overlook things that could spur positive change. Complicating matters, we also tend to view unexpected or unpleasant information as a threat and to shun it—a phenomenon psychologists call *motivated skepticism.*

In fact, research suggests, the manner in which we weigh evidence resembles the manner in which we weigh ourselves on a bathroom scale. If the scale delivers bad news, we hop off and get back on—perhaps the scale misfired or we misread the display. If it delivers good news, we assume it's correct and cheerfully head for the shower.

Here's a more scientific example. Two psychologists, Peter Ditto and David Lopez, asked study participants to evaluate a student's intelligence by reviewing information about him one piece at a time— similar to the way college admissions officers evaluate applicants. The information was quite negative. Subjects could stop going through it as soon as they'd reached a firm conclusion. When they had been primed to like the student (with a photo and some information provided before the evaluation), they turned over one card after another, searching for anything that would allow them to give a favorable rating. When they had been primed to dislike him, they turned over a few cards, shrugged, and called it a day.

By uncritically accepting information when it is consistent with what we believe and insisting on more when it isn't, we subtly stack the deck against good decisions.

Promoting Constructive Nonconformity

Few leaders actively encourage deviant behavior in their employees; most go to great lengths to get rid of it. Yet nonconformity promotes innovation, improves performance, and can enhance a person's standing more than conformity can. For example, research I conducted with Silvia Bellezza, of Columbia, and Anat Keinan, of Harvard, showed that observers judge a keynote speaker who wears red sneakers, a CEO who makes the rounds of Wall Street in a hoodie and jeans, and a presenter who creates her own PowerPoint template rather than using her company's as having higher status than counterparts who conform to business norms.

My research also shows that going against the crowd gives us confidence in our actions, which makes us feel unique and engaged and translates to higher performance and greater creativity. In one field study, I asked a group of employees to behave in nonconforming ways (speaking up if they disagreed with colleagues' decisions, expressing what they felt rather than what they thought they were expected to feel, and so on). I asked another group to behave in conforming ways, and a third group to do whatever its members usually did. After three weeks, those in the first group reported feeling more confident and engaged in their work than those in the other groups. They displayed more creativity in a task that was part of the study. And their supervisors gave them higher ratings on performance and innovativeness.

Six strategies can help leaders encourage constructive nonconformity in their organizations and themselves.

Step 1: Give Employees Opportunities to Be Themselves

Decades' worth of psychological research has shown that we feel accepted and believe that our views are more credible when our colleagues share them. But although conformity may make us feel good, it doesn't let us reap the benefits of authenticity. In one study Dan Cable, of London Business School, and Virginia Kay, then of the University of North Carolina at Chapel Hill, surveyed 154 recent MBA graduates who were four months into their jobs. Those who felt they could express their authentic selves at work were, on average, 16% more engaged and more committed to their organizations than those who felt they had to hide their authentic selves. In another study, Cable and Kay surveyed 2,700 teachers who had been working for a year and reviewed the performance ratings given by their supervisors. Teachers who said they could express their authentic selves received higher ratings than teachers who did not feel they could do so.

Here are some ways to help workers be true to themselves:

Encourage employees to reflect on what makes them feel authentic. This can be done from the very start of the employment relationship—during orientation. In a field study I conducted with

The perils of conformity

Organizations put tremendous pressure on employees to conform. In a recent survey of 2,087 US employees in a wide range of industries, nearly 49% agreed with the statement "I regularly feel pressure to conform in this organization."

This takes a heavy toll on individuals and enterprises alike. Employees who felt a need to conform reported a less positive work experience on several dimensions than did other employees, as shown by the average scores plotted below.

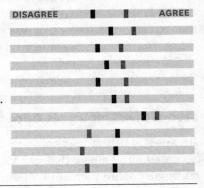

■ Regularly feels pressure to conform   ■ Doesn't regularly feel pressure to conform

- I can be myself at work.
- My organization fully uses my talents.
- I am committed to my organization.
- I am engaged in my work.
- I am satisfied with my job.
- I try to improve my job and my organization.
- I perform at a high level.
- I lack control over my job.
- I feel burned out.
- I would like to leave my organization.

DISAGREE — AGREE

Brad Staats, of the University of North Carolina at Chapel Hill, and Dan Cable, employees in the business-process-outsourcing division of the Indian IT company Wipro went through a slightly modified onboarding process. We gave them a half hour to think about what was unique about them, what made them authentic, and how they could bring out their authentic selves at work. Later we compared them with employees who had gone through Wipro's usual onboarding program, which allowed no time for such reflection. The employees in the first group had found ways to tailor their jobs so that they could be their true selves—for example, they exercised judgment when answering calls instead of rigidly following the company script. They were more engaged in their work, performed better, and were more likely to be with the company seven months later.

Leaders can also encourage this type of reflection once people are on the job. The start of a new year is a natural time for employees and their leaders to reflect on what makes them unique and authentic and how they can shape their jobs—even in small ways—to avoid conformity. Reflection can also be encouraged at other career points, such as a performance review, a promotion, or a transition into a new role.

Tell employees what job needs to be done rather than how to do it. When Colleen Barrett was executive vice president of Southwest Airlines, from 1990 to 2001, she established the goal of allowing employees to be themselves. For example, flight attendants were encouraged to deliver the legally required safety announcement in their own style and with humor. "We have always thought that your avocation can be your vocation so that you don't have to do any acting in your life when you leave home to go to work," she has said. This philosophy helped make Southwest a top industry performer in terms of passenger volume, profitability, customer satisfaction, and turnover.

Let employees solve problems on their own. Leaders can encourage authenticity by allowing workers to decide how to handle certain situations. For instance, in the 1990s British Airways got rid of its thick customer-service handbook and gave employees the freedom (within reason) to figure out how to deal with customer problems as they arose (see "Competing on Customer Service: An Interview with British Airways' Sir Colin Marshall," HBR, November–December 1995).

Another company that subscribes to this philosophy is Pal's Sudden Service, a fast-food chain in the southern United States. By implementing lean principles, including the idea that workers are empowered to call out and fix problems, Pal's has achieved impressive numbers: one car served at the drive-through every 18 seconds, one mistake in every 3,600 orders (the industry average is one in 15), customer satisfaction scores of 98%, and health inspection scores above 97%. Turnover at the assistant manager level is under 2%, and in three decades Pal's has lost only seven general managers—two of them to retirement. Annual turnover on the front lines is about 34%—half the industry average. Pal's trains its employees extensively: New frontline workers receive 135 hours of instruction, on average (the industry average is about two hours). As a result, employees are confident that they can solve problems on their own and can stop processes if something does not seem right. (They also know they can ask for help.) When I was conducting interviews for a case on Pal's, a general manager gave me an example of how he encourages frontline workers to make decisions themselves: "A 16-year-old [employee] shows me a hot dog bun with flour on it and asks me if it's OK. My response: 'Your call. Would you sell it?'"

Let employees define their missions. Morning Star, a California-based tomato processing company, has employees write "personal commercial mission statements" that reflect who they are and specify their goals for a given time period, ones that will contribute to the company's success. The statements are embedded in contracts known as "colleague letters of understanding," or CLOUs, which employees negotiate with coworkers, each spelling out how he or she will collaborate with others. The personal commercial mission of Morning Star's founder, Chris Rufer, is "to advance tomato technology to be the best in the world and operate these factories so they are pristine." That of one sales and marketing employee is "to indelibly mark 'Morning Star Tomato Products' on the tongue and brain of every commercial tomato product user." That of one employee in the shipping unit is "to reliably and efficiently provide our customers with marvelously attractive loads of desired product."

Step 2: Encourage Employees to Bring Out Their Signature Strengths

Michelangelo described sculpting as a process whereby the artist releases an ideal figure from the block of stone in which it slumbers. We all possess ideal forms, the signature strengths—being social connectors, for example, or being able to see the positive in any situation—that we use naturally in our lives. And we all have a drive to do what we do best and be recognized accordingly. A leader's task is to encourage employees to sculpt their jobs to bring out their strengths—and to sculpt his or her own job, too. The actions below can help.

Give employees opportunities to identify their strengths. In a research project I conducted with Dan Cable, Brad Staats, and the University of Michigan's Julia Lee, leaders of national and local government agencies across the globe reflected each morning on their signature strengths and how to use them. They also read descriptions of times when they were at their best, written by people in their personal and professional networks. These leaders displayed more engagement and innovative behavior than members of a control group, and their teams performed better.

Tailor jobs to employees' strengths. Facebook is known for hiring smart people regardless of the positions currently open in the company, gathering information about their strengths, and designing their jobs accordingly. Another example is Osteria Francescana, a Michelin three-star restaurant in Modena, Italy, that won first place in the 2016 World's 50 Best Restaurant awards. Most restaurants, especially top-ranked ones, observe a strict hierarchy, with specific titles for each position. But at Osteria Francescana, jobs and their attendant responsibilities are tailored to individual workers.

Discovering employees' strengths takes time and effort. Massimo Bottura, the owner and head chef, rotates interns through various positions for at least a few months so that he and his team can configure jobs to play to the newcomers' strengths. This ensures that employees land where they fit best.

If such a process is too ambitious for your organization, consider giving employees some freedom to choose responsibilities within their assigned roles.

Step 3: Question the Status Quo, and Encourage Employees to Do the Same

Although businesses can benefit from repeatable practices that ensure consistency, they can also stimulate employee engagement and innovation by questioning standard procedures—"the way we've always done it." Here are some proven tactics.

Ask "Why?" and "What if?" By regularly asking employees such questions, Max Zanardi, for several years the general manager of the Ritz-Carlton in Istanbul, creatively led them to redefine luxury by providing customers with authentic and unusual experiences. For example, employees had traditionally planted flowers each year on the terrace outside the hotel's restaurant. One day Zanardi asked, "Why do we always plant flowers? How about vegetables? What about herbs?" This resulted in a terrace garden featuring herbs and heirloom tomatoes used in the restaurant—things guests very much appreciated.

Leaders who question the status quo give employees reasons to stay engaged and often spark fresh ideas that can rejuvenate the business.

Stress that the company is not perfect. Ed Catmull, the cofounder and president of Pixar Animation Studios, worried that new hires would be too awed by Pixar's success to challenge existing practices (see "How Pixar Fosters Collective Creativity," HBR, September 2008). So during onboarding sessions, his speeches included examples of the company's mistakes. Emphasizing that we are all human and that the organization will never be perfect gives employees freedom to engage in constructive nonconformity.

Excel at the basics. Ensuring that employees have deep knowledge about the way things usually operate provides them with a foundation for constructively questioning the status quo. This philosophy underlies the many hours Pal's devotes to training: Company leaders want employees to be expert in all aspects of their work. Similarly, Bottura believes that to create innovative dishes, his chefs must be well versed in classic cooking techniques.

Step 4: Create Challenging Experiences

It's easy for workers to get bored and fall back on routine when their jobs involve little variety or challenge. And employees who find their work boring lack the motivation to perform well and creatively, whereas work that is challenging enhances their engagement. Research led by David H. Zald, of Vanderbilt University, shows that novel behavior, such as trying something new or risky, triggers the release of dopamine, a chemical that helps keep us motivated and eager to innovate.

Leaders can draw on the following tactics when structuring employees' jobs:

Maximize variety. This makes it less likely that employees will go on autopilot and more likely that they will come up with innovative ways to improve what they're doing. It also boosts performance, as Brad Staats and I found in our analysis of two and a half years' worth of transaction data from a Japanese bank department responsible for processing home loan applications. The mortgage line involved 17 distinct tasks, including scanning applications, comparing scanned documents to originals, entering application data into the computer system, assessing whether information complied with underwriting standards, and conducting credit checks. Workers who were assigned diverse tasks from day to day were more productive than others (as measured by the time taken to complete each task); the variety kept them motivated. This allowed the bank to process applications more quickly, increasing its competitiveness.

Variety can be ensured in a number of ways. Pal's rotates employees through tasks (taking orders, grilling, working the register, and so on) in a different order each day. Some companies forgo defined career trajectories and instead move employees through various positions within departments or teams over the course of months or years.

In addition to improving engagement, job rotation broadens individuals' skill sets, creating a more flexible workforce. This makes it easier to find substitutes if someone falls ill or abruptly quits and to shift people from tasks where they are no longer needed (see "Why 'Good Jobs' Are Good for Retailers," HBR, January–February 2012).

Continually inject novelty into work. Novelty is a powerful force. When something new happens at work, we pay attention, engage, and tend to remember it. We are less likely to take our work for granted when it continues to generate strong feelings. Novelty in one's job is more satisfying than stability.

So, how can leaders inject it into work? Bottura throws last-minute menu changes at his team to keep excitement high. At Pal's, employees learn the order of their tasks for the day only when they get to work.

Leaders can also introduce novelty by making sure that projects include a few people who are somewhat out of their comfort zone, or by periodically giving teams new challenges (for instance, asking them to deliver a product faster than in the past). They can assign employees to teams charged with designing a new work process or piloting a new service.

Identify opportunities for personal learning and growth. Giving people such experiences is an essential way to promote constructive nonconformity, research has shown. For instance, in a field study conducted at a global consulting firm, colleagues and I found that when onboarding didn't just focus on performance but also spotlighted opportunities for learning and growth, engagement and innovative behaviors were higher six months later. Companies often identify growth opportunities during performance reviews, of course, but there are many other ways to do so. Chefs at Osteria Francescana can accompany Bottura to cooking events that expose them to other countries, cuisines, traditions, arts, and culture—all potential sources of inspiration for new dishes. When I worked as a research consultant at Disney, in the summer of 2010, I learned that members of the Imagineering R&D group were encouraged to belong to professional societies, attend conferences, and publish in academic and professional journals. Companies can help pay for courses that may not strictly relate to employees' current jobs but would nonetheless expand their skill sets or fuel their curiosity.

Give employees responsibility and accountability. At Morning Star, if employees need new equipment to do their work—even something that costs thousands of dollars—they may buy it. If they see a process that would benefit from different skills, they may hire someone. They must consult colleagues who would be affected (other people who would use the equipment, say), but they don't need approval from above. Because there are no job titles at Morning Star, how employees influence others—and thus get work done—is determined mainly by how their colleagues perceive the quality of their decisions.

Step 5: Foster Broader Perspectives

We often focus so narrowly on our own point of view that we have trouble understanding others' experiences and perspectives. And as we assume high-level positions, research shows, our egocentric focus becomes stronger. Here are some ways to combat it:

Create opportunities for employees to view problems from multiple angles. We all tend to be self-serving in terms of how we process information and generate (or fail to generate) alternatives to the status quo. Leaders can help employees overcome this tendency by encouraging them to view problems from different perspectives. At the electronics manufacturer Sharp, an oft-repeated maxim is "Be dragonflies, not flatfish." Dragonflies have compound eyes that can take in multiple perspectives at once; flatfish have both eyes on the same side of the head and can see in only one direction at a time.

Jon Olinto and Anthony Ackil, the founders of the fast-casual restaurant chain b.good, require all employees (including managers) and franchisees to be trained in every job—from prep to grill to register. (Unlike Pal's, however, b.good does not rotate people through jobs each day.) Being exposed to different perspectives increases engagement and innovative behaviors, research has found.

Use language that reduces self-serving bias. To prevent their traders from letting success go to their heads when the market is booming, some Wall Street firms regularly remind them, "Don't confuse brains with a bull market." At GE, terms such as "planting seeds" (to describe making investments that will produce fruitful results even after the managers behind them have moved on to other jobs) have entered the lexicon (see "How GE Teaches Teams to Lead Change," HBR, January 2009).

Hire people with diverse perspectives. Decades' worth of research has found that working among people from a variety of cultures and backgrounds helps us see problems in new ways and consider ideas that might otherwise go unnoticed, and it fosters the kind of creativity that champions change. At Osteria Francescana the two sous-chefs are Kondo "Taka" Takahiko, from Japan, and Davide di Fabio, from Italy. They differ not only in country of origin but also in strengths and ways of thinking: Davide is comfortable with improvisation, for example, while Taka is obsessed with precision. Diversity in ways of thinking is a quality sought by Rachael Chong, the founder and CEO of the startup Catchafire. When interviewing job candidates, she describes potential challenges and carefully listens to see whether people come up with many possible solutions or get stuck on a single one. To promote innovation and new approaches, Ed Catmull hires prominent outsiders, gives them important roles, and publicly acclaims their contributions. But many organizations do just the opposite: hire people whose thinking mirrors that of the current management team.

Step 6: Voice and Encourage Dissenting Views

We often seek out and fasten on information that confirms our beliefs. Yet data that is inconsistent with our views and may even generate negative feelings (such as a sense of failure) can provide opportunities to improve our organizations and ourselves. Leaders can use a number of tactics to push employees out of their comfort zones.

Look for disconfirming evidence. Leaders shouldn't ask, "Who agrees with this course of action?" or "What information supports this view?" Instead they should ask, "What information suggests this might not be the right path to take?" Mellody Hobson, the president of Ariel Investments and the chair of the board of directors of DreamWorks Animation, regularly opens team meetings by reminding attendees that they don't need to be right; they need to bring up information that can help the team make the right decisions, which happens when members voice their concerns and disagree. At the Chicago Board of Trade, in-house investigators scrutinize trades that may violate exchange rules. To avoid bias in collecting information, they have been trained to ask open-ended interview questions, not ones that can be answered with a simple yes or no. Leaders can use a similar approach when discussing decisions. They should also take care not to depend on opinions but to assess whether the data supports or undermines the prevailing point of view.

Create dissent by default. Leaders can encourage debate during meetings by inviting individuals to take opposing points of view; they can also design processes to include dissent. When employees of Pal's suggest promising ideas for new menu items, the ideas are tested in three different stores: one whose owner-operator likes the idea ("the protagonist"), one whose owner-operator is skeptical ("the antagonist"), and one whose owner-operator has yet to form a strong opinion ("the neutral"). This ensures that dissenting views are aired and that they help inform the CEO's decisions about proposed items.

Identify courageous dissenters. Even if encouraged to push back, many timid or junior people won't. So make sure the team includes people you know will voice their concerns, writes Diana McLain Smith in *The Elephant in the Room: How Relationships Make or Break the Success of Leaders and Organizations*. Once the more reluctant employees see that opposing views are welcome, they will start to feel comfortable dissenting as well.

Striking the Right Balance

By adopting the strategies above, leaders can fight their own and their employees' tendency to conform when that would hurt the company's interests. But to strike the optimal balance between conformity and nonconformity, they must think carefully about the

Assessment: Are You a "Constructive Nonconformist"?

Find out how much of a rebel worker you are.

For decades, prevailing management wisdom has encouraged leaders to focus on designing efficient processes and getting employees to follow them. But conformity can hurt businesses. Innovation and high performance often result from behaviors that defy organizational norms—established ways of thinking and of doing things. How much does your company pressure you to conform? And are you succumbing to the pressure and hurting your chances of success? Take the following assessment (adapted from my ongoing research) to discover whether you're engaging in what I call constructive nonconformity: deviant behavior that benefits the organization.

When answering these questions, focus on the past month.	Never	Almost never	Some-times	Fairly often	Very often	Always
1. In the past month, how often have you refrained from opposing your team members just to avoid rocking the boat?	0	1	2	3	4	5
2. How often have you publicly supported ideas you privately disagreed with?	0	1	2	3	4	5
3. How often have you followed established rules or procedures, even though you suspected there was a better way to do things?	0	1	2	3	4	5
4. How often have you raised questions about the effectiveness of current processes or systems?	5	4	3	2	1	0
5. How often have you seen senior leaders challenge the status quo or ask employees to think outside the box?	5	4	3	2	1	0
6. How often have you felt pressured to conform to the cultural norms of your organization (how to dress, how to interact with others, how to do your work, and so on)?	0	1	2	3	4	5

When answering these questions, focus on the past month.	Never	Almost never	Some-times	Fairly often	Very often	Always
7. How often have you felt free to be yourself—to behave and express yourself in an authentic way?	5	4	3	2	1	0
8. How often have you been encouraged to solve problems on your own, without involving a supervisor?	5	4	3	2	1	0
9. How often has your job played to your strengths?	5	4	3	2	1	0
10. How often have you been challenged—urged to develop a new skill or to take on a task that pushed you out of your comfort zone?	5	4	3	2	1	0
11. How often have you sought information that was inconsistent with your views and might even prove you wrong?	5	4	3	2	1	0
12. How often have you and your team been encouraged to debate ideas or consider multiple perspectives before reaching a decision?	5	4	3	2	1	0

Score: 0–24 You're lucky: Your low score indicates that you are probably very engaged in your work, are performing at a high level, and are innovating frequently. Just make sure that you don't become complacent—the pressure to conform affects everyone. Keep being the rebel that you are!

Score: 25–30 Your score is average—and in this case, average is good. Scores in this range indicate that your ability to express yourself at work is at a healthy level, allowing you to be productive and innovative. To stay in this sweet spot, watch out for situations in which you feel pressured to conform.

Score: 31–39 Your higher-than-average score indicates a level of pressure that may be detrimental to your performance and your ability to innovate. You may also be disengaged. Try shaping your job in ways that allow you to be yourself and that bring out your talents and skills. Even small changes can let your authentic self shine through.

Score: 40–60 Your high score indicates an unproductive level of conformity. You're probably disengaged, and you're almost certainly having a hard time being your true self at work. It's critical that you find ways (big and small) to lower the pressure to conform, and that starts with allowing your authentic self to shine through. Act more like a rebel, and you and your organization will benefit.

boundaries within which employees will be free to deviate from the status quo. For instance, the way a manager leads her team can be up to her as long as her behavior is aligned with the company's purpose and values and she delivers on that purpose.

Morning Star's colleague letters of understanding provide such boundaries. They clearly state employees' goals and their responsibility to deliver on the organization's purpose but leave it up to individual workers to decide how to achieve those goals. Colleagues with whom an employee has negotiated a CLOU will let him know if his actions cross a line.

Brazil's Semco Group, a 3,000-employee conglomerate, similarly relies on peer pressure and other mechanisms to give employees considerable freedom while making sure they don't go overboard. The company has no job titles, dress code, or organizational charts. If you need a workspace, you reserve it in one of a few satellite offices scattered around São Paulo. Employees, including factory workers, set their own schedules and production quotas. They even choose the amount and form of their compensation. What prevents employees from taking advantage of this freedom? First, the company believes in transparency: All its financial information is public, so everyone knows what everyone else makes. People who pay themselves too much have to work with resentful colleagues. Second, employee compensation is tied directly to company profits, creating enormous peer pressure to keep budgets in line.

Ritz-Carlton, too, excels in balancing conformity and nonconformity. It depends on 3,000 standards developed over the years to ensure a consistent customer experience at all its hotels. These range from how to slice a lime to which toiletries to stock in the bathrooms. But employees have considerable freedom within those standards and can question them if they see ways to provide an even better customer experience. For instance, for many years the company has allowed staff members to spend up to $2,000 to address any customer complaint in the way they deem best. (Yes, that is $2,000 per employee per guest.) The hotel believes that business is most successful when employees have well-defined standards, understand the reasoning behind them, and are given autonomy in carrying them out.

Organizations, like individuals, can easily become complacent, especially when business is going well. Complacency often sets in because of too much conformity—stemming from peer pressure, acceptance of the status quo, and the interpretation of information in self-serving ways. The result is a workforce of people who feel they can't be themselves on the job, are bored, and don't consider others' points of view.

Constructive nonconformity can help companies avoid these problems. If leaders were to put just half the time they spend ensuring conformity into designing and installing mechanisms to encourage constructive deviance, employee engagement, productivity, and innovation would soar.

Further Reading

IN THE COURSE OF DEVELOPING the Big Idea on Rebel Talent (October–November 2016), HBR asked Francesca Gino to provide a portfolio of content that could further inspire, advise, and help develop your understanding of the topic. Gino's curated list of materials on rebel talent runs the gamut from classic HBR articles to novels and more.

HBR Articles

While studying leaders and organizations that attract, develop, and manage talent so as to spark engagement and creativity, I found many insights in the pages of HBR.

- **"How Pixar Fosters Collective Creativity,"** Ed Catmull, September 2008

- **"Are You a High Potential?"** Douglas A. Ready, Jay A. Conger, and Linda A. Hill, June 2010

- **"How to Hang On to Your High Potentials,"** Claudio Fernández-Aráoz, Boris Groysberg, and Nitin Nohria, October 2011

- **"How GE Teaches Teams to Lead Change,"** Steven Prokesch, January 2009

- **"Managing Without Managers,"** Ricardo Semler, September–October 1989

- **"Why My Former Employees Still Work for Me,"** Ricardo Semler, January–February 1994

Books

I've found inspiration in books from as far back as the 1950s that document how and why companies create pressure to conform and what can be done to combat it.

- *The Organization Man,* William H. Whyte, 1956
- *Reinventing Organizations: A Guide to Creating Organizations Inspired by the Next Stage of Human Consciousness,* Frederic Laloux, 2014
- *The Art of Being Unmistakable: A Collection of Essays About Making a Dent in the Universe,* Srinivas Rao, 2013
- *Bartleby, the Scrivener,* Herman Melville, 1853
- *Collective Genius: The Art and Practice of Leading Innovation,* Linda A. Hill, Greg Brandeau, Emily Truelove, and Kent Lineback, 2014

Case Studies

The best way to learn how to foster constructive nonconformity is to dig into how actual companies did so.

- **"Sun Hydraulics: Leading in Tough Times (A),"** Linda A. Hill and Jennifer M. Suesse, 2003
- **"Pal's Sudden Service—Scaling an Organizational Model to Drive Growth,"** Gary P. Pisano, Francesca Gino, and Bradley R. Staats, 2016
- **"The Morning Star Company: Self-Management at Work,"** Francesca Gino and Bradley R. Staats, 2013

Other Articles

- **"Monkeys Are Adept at Picking Up Social Cues, Research Shows,"** Pam Belluck, *New York Times*, 2013
- **"For Some Flight Attendants, Shtick Comes with the Safety Spiel,"** Zach Schonbrun, *New York Times*, 2016
- **"I'm Quite Eccentric Within Accepted Societal Norms,"** Martin Grossman, *The Onion*, 2007

Originally published in October–November 2016. Reprint H035GG

The Feedback Fallacy

by Marcus Buckingham and Ashley Goodall

THE DEBATE ABOUT FEEDBACK AT WORK isn't new. Since at least the middle of the last century, the question of how to get employees to improve has generated a good deal of opinion and research. But recently the discussion has taken on new intensity.

The ongoing experiment in "radical transparency" at Bridgewater Associates and the culture at Netflix, which the *Wall Street Journal* recently described as "encouraging harsh feedback" and subjecting workers to "intense and awkward" real-time 360s, are but two examples of the overriding belief that the way to increase performance in companies is through rigorous, frequent, candid, pervasive, and often critical feedback.

How should we give and receive feedback? we wonder. How much, and how often, and using which new app? And, given the hoopla over the approaches of Bridgewater and Netflix, how hard-edged and fearlessly candid should we be? Behind those questions, however, is another question that we're missing, and it's a crucial one. The search for ways to give and receive better feedback assumes that feedback is always useful. But the only reason we're pursuing it is to help people do better. And when we examine *that*—asking, *How can we help each person thrive and excel?*—we find that the answers take us in a different direction.

To be clear, instruction—telling people what steps to follow or what factual knowledge they're lacking—can be truly useful: That's why we have checklists in airplane cockpits and, more recently, in operating rooms. There is indeed a right way for a nurse to give an injection safely, and if you as a novice nurse miss one of the steps, or if you're unaware of critical facts about a patient's condition, then someone should tell you. But the occasions when the actions or knowledge necessary to minimally perform a job can be objectively defined in advance are rare and becoming rarer. What we mean by "feedback" is very different. Feedback is about telling people what we think of their performance and how they should do it better—whether they're giving an effective presentation, leading a team, or creating a strategy. And on that, the research is clear: Telling people what we think of their performance doesn't help them thrive and excel, and telling people how we think they should improve actually *hinders* learning.

Underpinning the current conviction that feedback is an unalloyed good are three theories that we in the business world commonly accept as truths. The first is that other people are more aware than you are of your weaknesses, and that the best way to help you, therefore, is for them to show you what you cannot see for yourself. We can call this our *theory of the source of truth*. You do not realize that your suit is shabby, that your presentation is boring, or that your voice is grating, so it is up to your colleagues to tell you as plainly as possible "where you stand." If they didn't, you would never know, and this would be bad.

The second belief is that the process of learning is like filling up an empty vessel: You lack certain abilities you need to acquire, so your colleagues should teach them to you. We can call this our *theory of learning*. If you're in sales, how can you possibly close deals if you don't learn the competency of "mirroring and matching" the prospect? If you're a teacher, how can you improve if you don't learn and practice the steps in the latest team-teaching technique or "flipped classroom" format? The thought is that you can't—and that you need feedback to develop the skills you're missing.

And the third belief is that great performance is universal, analyzable, and describable, and that once defined, it can be transferred from one person to another, regardless of who each individual is. Hence you can, with feedback about what excellence looks like,

Idea in Brief

The Challenge

Managers today are bombarded with calls to give feedback—constantly, directly, and critically. But it turns out that telling people what we think of their performance and how they can do better is not the best way to help them excel and, in fact, can hinder development.

The Reality

Research shows that, first, we aren't the reliable raters of other people's performance that we think we are; second, criticism inhibits the brain's ability to learn; and, third, excellence is idiosyncratic, can't be defined in advance, and isn't the opposite of failure. Managers can't "correct" a person's way to excellence.

The Solution

Managers need to help their team members see what's working, stopping them with a "Yes! That!" and sharing their experience of what the person did well.

understand where you fall short of this ideal and then strive to remedy your shortcomings. We can call this our *theory of excellence.* If you're a manager, your boss might show you the company's supervisor-behaviors model, hold you up against it, and tell you what you need to do to more closely hew to it. If you aspire to lead, your firm might use a 360-degree feedback tool to measure you against its predefined leadership competencies and then suggest various courses or experiences that will enable you to acquire the competencies that your results indicate you lack.

What these three theories have in common is self-centeredness: They take our own expertise and what we are sure is our colleagues' inexpertise as givens; they assume that my way is necessarily your way. But as it turns out, in extrapolating from what creates our own performance to what might create performance in others, we overreach.

Research reveals that none of these theories is true. The more we depend on them, and the more technology we base on them, the *less* learning and productivity we will get from others. To understand why and to see the path to a more effective way of improving performance, let's look more closely at each theory in turn.

The Source of Truth

The first problem with feedback is that humans are unreliable raters of other humans. Over the past 40 years psychometricians have shown in study after study that people don't have the objectivity to hold in their heads a stable definition of an abstract quality, such as *business acumen* or *assertiveness*, and then accurately evaluate someone else on it. Our evaluations are deeply colored by our own understanding of what we're rating others on, our own sense of what good looks like for a particular competency, our harshness or leniency as raters, and our own inherent and unconscious biases. This phenomenon is called the *idiosyncratic rater effect*, and it's large (more than half of your rating of someone else reflects your characteristics, not hers) and resilient (no training can lessen it). In other words, the research shows that feedback is more distortion than truth.

This is why, despite all the training available on how to *receive* feedback, it's such hard work: Recipients have to struggle through this forest of distortion in search of something that they recognize as themselves.

And because your feedback to others is always more you than them, it leads to systematic error, which is magnified when ratings are considered in aggregate. There are only two sorts of measurement error in the world: *random* error, which you can reduce by averaging many readings; and *systematic* error, which you can't. Unfortunately, we all seem to have left math class remembering the former and not the latter. We've built all our performance and leadership feedback tools as though assessment errors are random, and they're not. They're systematic.

Consider color blindness. If we ask a color-blind person to rate the redness of a particular rose, we won't trust his feedback—we know that he is incapable of seeing, let alone "rating," red. His error isn't random; it's predictable and explainable, and it stems from a flaw in his measurement system; hence, it's systematic. If we then decide to ask seven more color-blind people to rate the redness of our rose, their errors will be equally systematic, and averaging their ratings won't get us any closer to determining the actual redness of the rose.

In fact, it's worse than this. Adding up all the inaccurate redness ratings—"gray," "pretty gray," "whitish gray," "muddy brown," and so on—and averaging them leads us *further away* both from learning anything reliable about the individuals' personal experiences of the rose and from the actual truth of how red our rose really is.

What the research has revealed is that we're all color-blind when it comes to abstract attributes, such as *strategic thinking, potential,* and *political savvy.* Our inability to rate others on them is predictable and explainable—it is systematic. We cannot remove the error by adding more data inputs and averaging them out, and doing that actually makes the error bigger.

Worse still, although science has long since proven that we are color-blind, in the business world we assume we're clear-eyed. Deep down we don't think we make very many errors at all. We think we're reliable raters of others. We think we're a source of truth. We aren't. We're a source of error.

When a feedback instrument surveys eight colleagues about your business acumen, your score of 3.79 is far greater a distortion than if it simply surveyed one person about you—the 3.79 number is *all* noise, no signal. Given that (a) we're starting to see more of this sort of data-based feedback, (b) this data on you will likely be kept by your company for a very long time, and (c) it will be used to pay, promote, train, and deploy or fire you, you should be worried about just how fundamentally flawed it really is.

The only realm in which humans are an unimpeachable source of truth is that of their own feelings and experiences. Doctors have long known this. When they check up on you post-op, they'll ask, "On a scale of one to 10, with 10 being high, how would you rate your pain?" And if you say, "Five," the doctor may then prescribe all manner of treatments, but what she's unlikely to do is challenge you on your "five." It doesn't make sense, no matter how many operations she has done, to tell you your "five" is wrong, and that, actually, this morning your pain is a "three." It doesn't make sense to try to parse what you mean by "five," and whether any cultural differences might indicate that your "five" is not, in fact, a real "five." It doesn't make sense to hold calibration sessions with other doctors to ensure that your "five" is the same as the other "fives" in the rooms down the hall. Instead, she can be confident that you are the best judge of your pain and that all she can know for sure is that you will be feeling better when you rate your pain lower. Your rating is yours, not hers.

Just as your doctor doesn't know the truth of your pain, we don't know the truth about our colleagues, at least not in any objective way. You may read that workers today—especially Millennials—want to know where they stand. You may occasionally have team members ask you to tell them where they stand, objectively. You may feel that it's your duty to try to answer these questions. But you can't— none of us can. All we can do—and it's not nothing—is share our own feelings and experiences, our own reactions. Thus we can tell someone whether his voice grates *on us*; whether he's persuasive *to us*; whether his presentation is boring *to us*. We may not be able to tell him where he stands, but we can tell him where he stands *with us*. Those are our truths, not his. This is a humbler claim, but at least it's accurate.

How We Learn

Another of our collective theories is that feedback contains useful information, and that this information is the magic ingredient that will accelerate someone's learning. Again, the research points in the opposite direction. Learning is less a function of adding something that isn't there than it is of recognizing, reinforcing, and refining what already is. There are two reasons for this.

The first is that, neurologically, we grow more in our areas of greater ability (our strengths are our development areas). The brain continues to develop throughout life, but each person's does so differently. Because of your genetic inheritance and the oddities of your early childhood environment, your brain's wiring is utterly unique. Some parts of it have tight thickets of synaptic connections, while others are far less dense, and these patterns are different from one person to the next. According to brain science, people grow far more neurons and synaptic connections where they already have the most neurons and synaptic connections. In other words, each brain grows most where it's already strongest. As Joseph LeDoux, a professor of neuroscience at New York University, memorably described it, "Added connections are therefore more like new buds on a branch rather than new branches." Through this lens, learning looks a lot like building, little by little, on the unique patterns already there within you. Which in turn means learning has to start by finding and understanding those patterns—your patterns, not someone else's.

Second, getting attention to our strengths from others catalyzes learning, whereas attention to our weaknesses smothers it. Neurological science also shows what happens to us when other people focus on what's working within us instead of remediating what isn't. In one experiment scientists split students into two groups. To one group they gave positive coaching, asking the students about their dreams and how they'd go about achieving them. The scientists probed the other group about homework and what the students thought they were doing wrong and needed to fix. While those conversations were happening, the scientists hooked each student up to a functional magnetic resonance imaging machine to see which parts of the brain were most activated in response to these different sorts of attention.

In the brains of the students asked about what they needed to correct, the sympathetic nervous system lit up. This is the "fight or flight" system, which mutes the other parts of the brain and allows us to focus only on the information most necessary to survive. Your brain responds to critical feedback as a threat and narrows its activity. The strong negative emotion produced by criticism "inhibits access to existing neural circuits and invokes cognitive, emotional, and perceptual impairment," psychology and business professor Richard Boyatzis said in summarizing the researchers' findings.

Focusing people on their shortcomings or gaps doesn't enable learning. It impairs it.

In the students who focused on their dreams and how they might achieve them, the sympathetic nervous system was not activated. What lit up instead was the parasympathetic nervous system, sometimes referred to as the "rest and digest" system. To quote Boyatzis again: "The parasympathetic nervous system . . . stimulates adult

41

neurogenesis (i.e., growth of new neurons) . . ., a sense of well-being, better immune system functioning, and cognitive, emotional, and perceptual openness."

What findings such as these show us is, first, that learning happens when we see how we might do something better by adding some new nuance or expansion to our own understanding. Learning rests on our grasp of what we're doing well, not on what we're doing poorly, and certainly not on someone else's sense of what we're doing poorly. And second, that we learn most when someone else pays attention to what's working within us and asks us to cultivate it intelligently. We're often told that the key to learning is to get out of our comfort zones, but these findings contradict that particular chestnut: Take us very far out of our comfort zones, and our brains stop paying attention to anything other than surviving the experience. It's clear that we learn most in our comfort zones, because that's where our neural pathways are most concentrated. It's where we're most open to possibility, most creative, insightful, and productive. That's where feedback must meet us—in our moments of flow.

Excellence

We spend the bulk of our working lives pursuing excellence in the belief that while defining it is easy, the really hard part is codifying how we and everyone else on our team should get there. We've got it backward: Excellence in any endeavor is almost impossible to define, and yet getting there, for each of us, is relatively easy.

Excellence is idiosyncratic. Take funniness—the ability to make others laugh. If you watch early Steve Martin clips, you might land on the idea that excellence at it means strumming a banjo, waggling your knees, and wailing, "I'm a wild and crazy guy!" But watch Jerry Seinfeld, and you might conclude that it means talking about nothing in a slightly annoyed, exasperated tone. And if you watch Sarah Silverman, you might think to yourself, no, it's being caustic, blunt, and rude in an incongruously affectless way. At this point you may begin to perceive the truth that "funny" is inherent to the person.

Watch an NBA game, and you may think to yourself, "Yes, most of them are tall and athletic, but boy, not only does each player have a different role on the team, but even the players in the same role on the same team seem to do it differently." Examine something as specific and as limited as the free throws awarded after fouls, and you'll learn that not only do the top two free-throw shooters in history have utterly different styles, but one of them, Rick Barry—the best ever on the day he retired (look him up)—didn't even throw overhand.

Excellence seems to be inextricably and wonderfully intertwined with whoever demonstrates it. Each person's version of it is uniquely shaped and is an expression of that person's individuality. Which means that, for each of us, excellence is easy, in that it is a natural, fluid, and intelligent expression of our best extremes. It can be cultivated, but it's unforced.

Excellence is also not the opposite of failure. But in virtually all aspects of human endeavor, people assume that it is and that if they study what leads to pathological functioning and do the reverse—or replace what they found missing—they can create optimal functioning. That assumption is flawed. Study disease and you will learn a lot about disease and precious little about health. Eradicating depression will get you no closer to joy. Divorce is mute on the topic of happy marriage. Exit interviews with employees who leave tell you nothing about why others stay. If you study failure, you'll learn a lot about failure but nothing about how to achieve excellence. Excellence has its own pattern.

And it's even more problematic than that. Excellence and failure often have a lot in common. So if you study ineffective leaders and observe that they have big egos, and then argue that good leaders should not have big egos, you will lead people astray. Why? Because when you do personality assessments with highly effective leaders, you discover that they have very strong egos as well. Telling someone that you must lose your ego to be a good leader is flawed advice. Likewise, if you study poor salespeople, discover that they take rejection personally, and then tell a budding salesperson to avoid doing the same, your advice will be misguided. Why? Because rigorous studies of the best salespeople reveal that they take rejection deeply personally, too.

As it happens, you find that effective leaders put their egos in the service of others, not themselves, and that effective salespeople take rejection personally because they are personally invested in the sale—but the point is that you will never find these things out by studying *ineffective* performance.

Since excellence is idiosyncratic and cannot be learned by studying failure, we can never help another person succeed by holding her performance up against a prefabricated model of excellence, giving her feedback on where she misses the model, and telling her to plug the gaps. That approach will only ever get her to adequate performance. Point out the grammatical flaws in an essay, ask the writer to fix the flaws, and while you may get an essay with good grammar, you won't get a piece of writing that transports the reader. Show a new teacher when her students lost interest and tell her what to do to fix this, and while you may now have a teacher whose students don't fall asleep in class, you won't have one whose students necessarily learn any more.

How to Help People Excel

If we continue to spend our time identifying failure as we see it and giving people feedback about how to avoid it, we'll languish in the business of adequacy. To get into the excellence business we need some new techniques:

Look for outcomes

Excellence is an outcome, so take note of when a prospect leans into a sales pitch, a project runs smoothly, or an angry customer suddenly calms down. Then turn to the team member who created the outcome and say, "That! Yes, that!" By doing this, you'll stop the flow of work for a moment and pull your colleague's attention back toward something she just did that really worked.

There's a story about how legendary Dallas Cowboys coach Tom Landry turned around his struggling team. While the other teams were reviewing missed tackles and dropped balls, Landry instead

The Right Way to Help Colleagues Excel

IF YOU WANT to get into the excellence business, here are some examples of language to try.

Instead of	Try
Can I give you some feedback?	Here's my reaction.
Good job!	Here are three things that really worked for me. What was going through your mind when you did them?
Here's what you should do.	Here's what I would do.
Here's where you need to improve.	Here's what worked best for me, and here's why.
That didn't really work.	When you did x, I felt y or I didn't get that.
You need to improve your communication skills.	Here's exactly where you started to lose me.
You need to be more responsive.	When I don't hear from you, I worry that we're not on the same page.
You lack strategic thinking.	I'm struggling to understand your plan.
You should do x [in response to a request for advice].	What do you feel you're struggling with, and what have you done in the past that's worked in a similar situation?

combed through footage of previous games and created for each player a highlight reel of when he had done something easily, naturally, and effectively. Landry reasoned that while the number of wrong ways to do something was infinite, the number of right ways, for any particular player, was not. It was knowable, and the best way to discover it was to look at plays where that person had done it excellently. From now on, he told each team member, "we only replay your winning plays."

Now on one level he was doing this to make his team members feel better about themselves because he knew the power of praise. But according to the story, Landry wasn't nearly as interested in praise as he was in learning. His instincts told him that each person would improve his performance most if he could see, in slow motion, what his own personal version of excellence looked like.

You can do the same. Whenever you see one of your people do something that worked for you, that rocked your world just a little, stop for a minute and highlight it. By helping your team member recognize what excellence looks like for her—by saying, "That! Yes, that!"—you're offering her the chance to gain an insight; you're highlighting a pattern that is already there within her so that she can recognize it, anchor it, re-create it, and refine it. That is learning.

Replay your instinctive reactions

Unlike Landry, you're not going to be able to videotape your people. Instead, learn how to replay to them your own personal reactions. The key is not to tell someone how well she's performed or how good she is. While simple praise isn't a bad thing, you are by no means the authority on what objectively good performance is, and instinctively she knows this. Instead, describe what you experienced when her moment of excellence caught your attention. There's nothing more believable and more authoritative than sharing what you saw from her and how it made you feel. Use phrases such as "This is how that came across for me," or "This is what that made me think," or even just "Did you see what you did there?" Those are your reactions—they are your truth—and when you relay them in specific detail, you aren't judging or rating or fixing her; you're simply reflecting to her the unique "dent" she just made in the world, as seen through your eyes. And precisely because it isn't a judgment or a rating, it is at once more humble and more powerful.

On the flip side, if you're the team member, whenever your team leader catches you doing something right, ask her to pause and describe her reaction to you. If she says, "Good job!" ask, "Which bit? What did you see that seemed to work well?" Again, the point of this isn't to pile on the praise. The point is to explore the nature of excellence, and this is surely a better object for all the energy currently being pointed at "radical transparency" and the like. We're so close to our own performance that it's hard to get perspective on it and see its patterns and components. Ask for your leader's help in rendering the unconscious, conscious—so that you can understand it, improve at it, and, most important, do it again.

Never lose sight of your highest-priority interrupt

In computing, a high-priority interrupt happens when something requires a computer processor's immediate attention, and the machine halts normal operations and jumps the urgent issue to the head of the processing queue. Like computer processors, team leaders have quite a few things that demand their attention and force them to act. Many of them are problems. If you see something go off the rails—a poorly handled call, a missed meeting, a project gone awry—the instinct will kick in to stop everything to tell someone what she did wrong and what she needs to do to fix it. This instinct is by no means misguided: If your team member screws something up, you have to deal with it. But remember that when you do, you're merely remediating—and that remediating not only inhibits learning but also gets you no closer to excellent performance. As we've seen, conjuring excellence from your team members requires a different focus from you. If you see somebody doing something that really works, stopping her and dissecting it with her isn't only a high-priority interrupt, it is your *highest*-priority interrupt. As you replay each small moment of excellence to your team member, you'll ease her into the "rest and digest" state of mind. Her understanding of what excellence looks and feels like within her will become more vivid, her brain will become more receptive to new information and will make connections to other inputs found in other regions of her brain, and she will learn and grow and get better.

Explore the present, past, and future

When people come to you asking for feedback on their performance or what they might need to fix to get promoted, try this:

Start with the *present*. If a team member approaches you with a problem, he's dealing with it *now*. He's feeling weak or challenged, and you have to address that. But rather than tackling the problem head-on, ask your colleague to tell you three things that are working for him *right now*. These things might be related to the situation or entirely separate. They might be significant or trivial. Just ask the question, and you're priming him with oxytocin—which is sometimes called the "love drug" but which here is better thought of as the "creativity drug." Getting him to think about specific things that are going well will alter his brain chemistry so that he can be open to new solutions and new ways of thinking or acting.

Next, go to the *past*. Ask him, "When you had a problem like this in the past, what did you do that worked?" Much of our life happens in patterns, so it's highly likely that he has encountered this problem at least a few times before. On one of those occasions he will almost certainly have found some way forward, some action or insight or connection that enabled him to move out of the mess. Get him thinking about that and seeing it in his mind's eye: what he actually felt and did, and what happened next.

Finally, turn to the *future*. Ask your team member, "What do you already know you need to do? What do you already know works in this situation?" By all means offer up one or two of your own experiences to see if they might clarify his own. But operate under the assumption that he already knows the solution—you're just helping him recognize it.

The emphasis here should not be on whys—"Why didn't that work?" "Why do you think you should do that?"—because those lead both of you into a fuzzy world of conjecture and concepts. Instead, focus on the whats—"What do you actually want to have happen?" "What are a couple of actions you could take right now?" These sorts of questions yield concrete answers, in which your colleague can find his actual self doing actual things in the near-term future.

How to give people feedback is one of the hottest topics in business today. The arguments for radical candor and unvarnished and pervasive transparency have a swagger to them, almost as if to imply that only the finest and bravest of us can face these truths with nerveless self-assurance, that those of us who recoil at the thought of working in a climate of continual judgment are condemned to mediocrity, and that as leaders our ability to look our colleagues squarely in the eye and lay out their faults without blinking is a measure of our integrity.

But at best, this fetish with feedback is good only for correcting mistakes—in the rare cases where the right steps are known and can be evaluated objectively. And at worst, it's toxic, because what we want from our people—and from ourselves—is not, for the most part, tidy adherence to a procedure agreed upon in advance or, for that matter, the ability to expose one another's flaws. It's that people contribute their own unique and growing talents to a common good, when that good is ever-evolving, when we are, for all the right reasons, making it up as we go along. Feedback has nothing to offer to that.

We humans do not do well when someone whose intentions are unclear tells us where we stand, how good we "really" are, and what we must do to fix ourselves. We excel *only* when people who know us and care about us tell us what they experience and what they feel, and in particular when they see something within us that really works.

Originally published in March–April 2019. Reprint R1902G

The Power of Small Wins

by Teresa M. Amabile and Steven J. Kramer

WHAT IS THE BEST WAY to drive innovative work inside organizations? Important clues hide in the stories of world-renowned creators. It turns out that ordinary *scientists*, *marketers*, *programmers*, and other unsung knowledge workers, whose jobs require creative productivity every day, have more in common with famous innovators than most managers realize. The workday events that ignite their emotions, fuel their motivation, and trigger their perceptions are fundamentally the same.

The Double Helix, James Watson's 1968 memoir about discovering the structure of DNA, describes the roller coaster of emotions he and Francis Crick experienced through the progress and setbacks of the work that eventually earned them the Nobel Prize. After the excitement of their first attempt to build a DNA model, Watson and Crick noticed some serious flaws. According to Watson, "Our first minutes with the models . . . were not joyous." Later that evening, "a shape began to emerge which brought back our spirits." But when they showed their "breakthrough" to colleagues, they found that their model would not work. Dark days of doubt and ebbing motivation followed. When the duo finally had their bona fide breakthrough, and their colleagues found no fault with it, Watson wrote, "My morale skyrocketed, for I suspected that we now had the answer to the riddle." Watson and Crick were so driven by this success that they practically lived in the lab, trying to complete the work.

Throughout these episodes, Watson and Crick's progress—or lack thereof—ruled their reactions. In our recent research on creative work inside businesses, we stumbled upon a remarkably similar phenomenon. Through exhaustive analysis of diaries kept by knowledge workers, we discovered the *progress principle*: Of all the things that can boost emotions, motivation, and perceptions during a workday, the single most important is making progress in meaningful work. And the more frequently people experience that sense of progress, the more likely they are to be creatively productive in the long run. Whether they are trying to solve a major scientific mystery or simply produce a high-quality product or service, everyday progress—even a small win—can make all the difference in how they feel and perform.

The power of progress is fundamental to human nature, but few managers understand it or know how to leverage progress to boost motivation. In fact, work motivation has been a subject of longstanding debate. In a survey asking about the keys to motivating workers, we found that some managers ranked recognition for good work as most important, while others put more stock in tangible incentives. Some focused on the value of interpersonal support, while still others thought clear goals were the answer. Interestingly, very few of our surveyed managers ranked progress first. (See the sidebar "A Surprise for Managers.")

If you are a manager, the progress principle holds clear implications for where to focus your efforts. It suggests that you have more influence than you may realize over employees' well-being, motivation, and creative output. Knowing what serves to catalyze and nourish progress—and what does the opposite—turns out to be the key to effectively managing people and their work.

In this article, we share what we have learned about the power of progress and how managers can leverage it. We spell out how a focus on progress translates into concrete managerial actions and provide a checklist to help make such behaviors habitual. But to clarify why those actions are so potent, we first describe our research and what the knowledge workers' diaries revealed about their *inner work lives*.

Idea in Brief

What could be more important for managers than increasing their teams' productivity? Yet most managers labor under misconceptions about what motivates employees—particularly knowledge workers—to do their best work.

On the basis of more than a decade of research, which included a deep analysis of daily diaries kept by teammates on creative projects, the authors clarify the matter once and for all: What motivates people on a day-to-day basis is the sense that they are making progress.

Managers who take this finding to heart will easily see the corollary: The best thing they can do for their people is provide the catalysts and nourishers that allow projects to move forward while removing the obstacles and toxins that result in setbacks. That is easily said, but for most managers it will require a new perspective and new behaviors. A simple checklist, consulted daily, can help make those habitual.

Inner Work Life and Performance

For nearly 15 years, we have been studying the psychological experiences and the performance of people doing complex work inside organizations. Early on, we realized that a central driver of creative, productive performance was the quality of a person's inner work life—the mix of emotions, motivations, and perceptions over the course of a workday. How happy workers feel; how motivated they are by an intrinsic interest in the work; how positively they view their organization, their management, their team, their work, and themselves—all these combine either to push them to higher levels of achievement or to drag them down.

To understand such interior dynamics better, we asked members of project teams to respond individually to an end-of-day e-mail survey during the course of the project—just over four months, on average. (For more on this research, see our article "Inner Work Life: Understanding the Subtext of Business Performance," HBR, May 2007.) The projects—inventing kitchen gadgets, managing product lines of cleaning tools, and solving complex IT problems for a hotel empire, for example—all involved creativity. The daily survey inquired about participants' emotions and moods, motivation

A Surprise for Managers

IN A 1968 ISSUE OF HBR, Frederick Herzberg published a now-classic article titled "One More Time: How Do You Motivate Employees?" Our findings are consistent with his message: People are most satisfied with their jobs (and therefore most motivated) when those jobs give them the opportunity to experience achievement.

The diary research we describe in this article—in which we microscopically examined the events of thousands of workdays, in real time—uncovered the mechanism underlying the sense of achievement: making consistent, meaningful progress.

But managers seem not to have taken Herzberg's lesson to heart. To assess contemporary awareness of the importance of daily work progress, we recently administered a survey to 669 managers of varying levels from dozens of companies around the world. We asked about the managerial tools that can affect employees' motivation and emotions. The respondents ranked five tools—support for making progress in the work, recognition for good work, incentives, interpersonal support, and clear goals—in order of importance.

Fully 95% of the managers who took our survey would probably be surprised to learn that supporting progress is the primary way to elevate motivation—because that's the percentage that failed to rank progress number one. In fact, only 35 managers ranked progress as the number one motivator—a mere 5%. The vast majority of respondents ranked support for making progress dead last as a motivator and third as an influence on emotion. They ranked "recognition for good work (either public or private)" as the most important factor in motivating workers and making them happy. In our diary study, recognition certainly did boost inner work life. But it wasn't nearly as prominent as progress. Besides, without work achievements, there is little to recognize.

---

levels, and perceptions of the work environment that day, as well as what work they did and what events stood out in their minds.

Twenty-six project teams from seven companies participated, comprising 238 individuals. This yielded nearly 12,000 diary entries. Naturally, every individual in our population experienced ups and downs. Our goal was to discover the states of inner work life and the workday events that correlated with the highest levels of creative output.

In a dramatic rebuttal to the commonplace claim that high pressure and fear spur achievement, we found that, at least in the realm of knowledge work, people are more creative and productive when their inner work lives are positive—when they feel happy, are intrinsically motivated by the work itself, and have positive perceptions of their colleagues and the organization. Moreover, in those positive states, people are more committed to the work and more collegial toward those around them. Inner work life, we saw, can fluctuate from one day to the next—sometimes wildly—and performance along with it. A person's inner work life on a given day fuels his or her performance for the day and can even affect performance the *next* day.

Once this *inner work life effect* became clear, our inquiry turned to whether and how managerial action could set it in motion. What events could evoke positive or negative emotions, motivations, and perceptions? The answers were tucked within our research participants' diary entries. There are predictable triggers that inflate or deflate inner work life, and, even accounting for variation among individuals, they are pretty much the same for everyone.

The Power of Progress

Our hunt for inner work life triggers led us to the progress principle. When we compared our research participants' best and worst days (based on their overall mood, specific emotions, and motivation levels), we found that the most common event triggering a "best day" was any progress in the work by the individual or the team. The most common event triggering a "worst day" was a setback.

Consider, for example, how progress relates to one component of inner work life: overall mood ratings. Steps forward occurred on 76% of people's best-mood days. By contrast, setbacks occurred on only 13% of those days. (See the exhibit "What happens on good days and bad days?")

Two other types of inner work life triggers also occur frequently on best days: *Catalysts*, actions that directly support work, including help from a person or group, and *nourishers*, events such as shows of respect and words of encouragement. Each has an opposite: *Inhibitors*, actions that fail to support or actively hinder work, and *toxins*, discouraging or undermining events. Whereas catalysts and inhibitors are directed

What happens on good days and bad days?

Progress—even a small step forward—occurs on many of the days people report being in a good mood. Events on bad days—setbacks and other hindrances—are nearly the mirror image of those on good days.

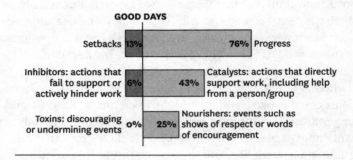

GOOD DAYS

| Setbacks | 13% | | 76% | Progress |

Inhibitors: actions that fail to support or actively hinder work — 6% — 43% — Catalysts: actions that directly support work, including help from a person/group

Toxins: discouraging or undermining events — 0% — 25% — Nourishers: events such as shows of respect or words of encouragement

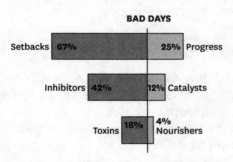

BAD DAYS

Setbacks — 67% — 25% Progress

Inhibitors — 42% — 12% Catalysts

Toxins — 18% — 4% Nourishers

at the project, nourishers and toxins are directed at the person. Like setbacks, inhibitors and toxins are rare on days of great inner work life.

Events on worst-mood days are nearly the mirror image of those on best-mood days (see the exhibit "What happens on good days and bad days?"). Here, setbacks predominated, occurring on 67% of those days; progress occurred on only 25% of them. Inhibitors and toxins also marked many worst-mood days, and catalysts and nourishers were rare.

This is the progress principle made visible: If a person is motivated and happy at the end of the workday, it's a good bet that he or she made some progress. If the person drags out of the office disengaged and joyless, a setback is most likely to blame.

When we analyzed all 12,000 daily surveys filled out by our participants, we discovered that progress and setbacks influence all three aspects of inner work life. On days when they made progress, our participants reported more positive *emotions*. They not only were in a more upbeat mood in general but also expressed more joy, warmth, and pride. When they suffered setbacks, they experienced more frustration, fear, and sadness.

Motivations were also affected: On progress days, people were more intrinsically motivated—by interest in and enjoyment of the work itself. On setback days, they were not only less intrinsically motivated but also less extrinsically motivated by recognition. Apparently, setbacks can lead a person to feel generally apathetic and disinclined to do the work at all.

Perceptions differed in many ways, too. On progress days, people perceived significantly more positive challenge in their work. They saw their teams as more mutually supportive and reported more positive interactions between the teams and their supervisors. On a number of dimensions, perceptions suffered when people encountered setbacks. They found less positive challenge in the work, felt that they had less freedom in carrying it out, and reported that they had insufficient resources. On setback days, participants perceived both their teams and their supervisors as less supportive.

To be sure, our analyses establish correlations but do not prove causality. Were these changes in inner work life the result of progress and setbacks, or was the effect the other way around? The numbers alone cannot answer that. However, we do know, from reading thousands of diary entries, that more-positive perceptions, a sense of accomplishment, satisfaction, happiness, and even elation often followed progress. Here's a typical post-progress entry, from a programmer: "I smashed that bug that's been frustrating me for almost a calendar week. That may not be an event to you, but I live a very drab life, so I'm all hyped."

Likewise, we saw that deteriorating perceptions, frustration, sadness, and even disgust often followed setbacks. As another participant, a product marketer, wrote, "We spent a lot of time updating the Cost Reduction project list, and after tallying all the numbers, we are still coming up short of our goal. It is discouraging to not be able to hit it after all the time spent and hard work."

Almost certainly, the causality goes both ways, and managers can use this feedback loop between progress and inner work life to support both.

Minor Milestones

When we think about progress, we often imagine how good it feels to achieve a long-term goal or experience a major breakthrough. These big wins are great—but they are relatively rare. The good news is that even small wins can boost inner work life tremendously. Many of the progress events our research participants reported represented only minor steps forward. Yet they often evoked outsize positive reactions. Consider this diary entry from a programmer in a high-tech company, which was accompanied by very positive self-ratings of her emotions, motivations, and perceptions that day: "I figured out why something was not working correctly. I felt relieved and happy because this was a minor milestone for me."

Even ordinary, incremental progress can increase people's engagement in the work and their happiness during the workday. Across all types of events our participants reported, a notable proportion (28%) of incidents that had a minor impact on the project had a major impact on people's feelings about it. Because inner work life has such a potent effect on creativity and productivity, and because small but consistent steps forward, shared by many people, can accumulate into excellent execution, progress events that often go unnoticed are critical to the overall performance of organizations.

Unfortunately, there is a flip side. Small losses or setbacks can have an extremely negative effect on inner work life. In fact, our study and research by others show that negative events can have a more powerful impact than positive ones. Consequently, it is especially important for managers to minimize daily hassles.

Progress in Meaningful Work

We've shown how gratifying it is for workers when they are able to chip away at a goal, but recall what we said earlier: The key to motivating performance is supporting progress in *meaningful* work. Making headway boosts your inner work life, but only if the work matters to you.

Think of the most boring job you've ever had. Many people nominate their first job as a teenager—washing pots and pans in a restaurant kitchen, for example, or checking coats at a museum. In jobs like those, the power of progress seems elusive. No matter how hard you work, there are always more pots to wash and coats to check; only punching the time clock at the end of the day or getting the paycheck at the end of the week yields a sense of accomplishment.

In jobs with much more challenge and room for creativity, like the ones our research participants had, simply "making progress"— getting tasks done—doesn't guarantee a good inner work life, either. You may have experienced this rude fact in your own job, on days (or in projects) when you felt demotivated, devalued, and frustrated, even though you worked hard and got things done. The likely cause is your perception of the completed tasks as peripheral or irrelevant. For the progress principle to operate, the work must be meaningful to the person doing it.

In 1983, Steve Jobs was trying to entice John Sculley to leave a wildly successful career at PepsiCo to become Apple's new CEO. Jobs reportedly asked him, "Do you want to spend the rest of your life selling sugared water or do you want a chance to change the world?" In making his pitch, Jobs leveraged a potent psychological force: the deep-seated human desire to do meaningful work.

Fortunately, to feel meaningful, work doesn't have to involve putting the first personal computers in the hands of ordinary people, or alleviating poverty, or helping to cure cancer. Work with less profound importance to society can matter if it contributes value to something or someone important to the worker. Meaning can be as simple as making a useful and high-quality product for a customer or providing a genuine service for a community. It can be supporting a colleague

How Work Gets Stripped of Its Meaning

DIARY ENTRIES FROM 238 KNOWLEDGE WORKERS who were members of creative project teams revealed four primary ways in which managers unwittingly drain work of its meaning.

1. **Managers may dismiss the importance of employees' work or ideas.** Consider the case of Richard, a senior lab technician at a chemical company, who found meaning in helping his new-product development team solve complex technical problems. However, in team meetings over the course of a three-week period, Richard perceived that his team leader was ignoring his suggestions and those of his teammates. As a result, he felt that his contributions were not meaningful, and his spirits flagged. When at last he believed that he was again making a substantive contribution to the success of the project, his mood improved dramatically:

   > I felt much better at today's team meeting. I felt that my opinions and information were important to the project and that we have made some progress.

2. **They may destroy employees' sense of ownership of their work.** Frequent and abrupt reassignments often have this effect. This happened repeatedly to the members of a product development team in a giant consumer products company, as described by team member Bruce:

   > As I've been handing over some projects, I do realize that I don't like to give them up. Especially when you have been with them from the

---

or boosting an organization's profits by reducing inefficiencies in a production process. Whether the goals are lofty or modest, as long as they are meaningful to the worker and it is clear how his or her efforts contribute to them, progress toward them can galvanize inner work life.

In principle, managers shouldn't have to go to extraordinary lengths to infuse jobs with meaning. Most jobs in modern organizations are potentially meaningful for the people doing them. However, managers can make sure that employees know just how their work is contributing. And, most important, they can avoid actions that negate its value. (See the sidebar "How Work Gets Stripped of Its Meaning.") All the participants in our research were doing work that should have been meaningful; no one was washing pots or check-start and are nearly to the end. You lose ownership. This happens to us way too often.

3. **Managers may send the message that the work employees are doing will never see the light of day.** They can signal this—unintentionally—by shifting their priorities or changing their minds about how something should be done. We saw the latter in an internet technology company after user-interface developer Burt had spent weeks designing seamless transitions for non-English-speaking users. Not surprisingly, Burt's mood was seriously marred on the day he reported this incident:

> Other options for the international [interfaces] were [given] to the team during a team meeting, which could render the work I am doing useless.

4. **They may neglect to inform employees about unexpected changes in a customer's priorities.** Often, this arises from poor customer management or inadequate communication within the company. For example, Stuart, a data transformation expert at an IT company, reported deep frustration and low motivation on the day he learned that weeks of the team's hard work might have been for naught:

> Found out that there is a strong possibility that the project may not be going forward, due to a shift in the client's agenda. Therefore, there is a strong possibility that all the time and effort put into the project was a waste of our time.

ing coats. Shockingly often, however, we saw potentially important, challenging work losing its power to inspire.

Supporting Progress: Catalysts and Nourishers

What can managers do to ensure that people are motivated, committed, and happy? How can they support workers' daily progress? They can use catalysts and nourishers, the other kinds of frequent "best day" events we discovered.

Catalysts are actions that support work. They include setting clear goals, allowing autonomy, providing sufficient resources and time, helping with the work, openly learning from problems and successes, and allowing a free exchange of ideas. Their opposites, inhibitors, include failing to provide support and actively interfering with the work. Because of their impact on progress, catalysts and inhibitors ultimately affect inner work life. But they also have a more immediate impact: When people realize that they have clear and meaningful goals, sufficient resources, helpful colleagues, and so on, they get an instant boost to their emotions, their motivation to do a great job, and their perceptions of the work and the organization.

Nourishers are acts of interpersonal support, such as respect and recognition, encouragement, emotional comfort, and opportunities for affiliation. Toxins, their opposites, include disrespect, discouragement, disregard for emotions, and interpersonal conflict. For good and for ill, nourishers and toxins affect inner work life directly and immediately.

Catalysts and nourishers—and their opposites—can alter the meaningfulness of work by shifting people's perceptions of their jobs and even themselves. For instance, when a manager makes sure that people have the resources they need, it signals to them that what they are doing is important and valuable. When managers recognize people for the work they do, it signals that they are important to the organization. In this way, catalysts and nourishers can lend greater meaning to the work—and amplify the operation of the progress principle.

The managerial actions that constitute catalysts and nourishers are not particularly mysterious; they may sound like Management 101, if not just common sense and common decency. But our diary study reminded us how often they are ignored or forgotten. Even some of the more attentive managers in the companies we studied did not consistently provide catalysts and nourishers. For example, a supply-chain specialist named Michael was, in many ways and on most days, an excellent subteam manager. But he was occasionally so overwhelmed that he became toxic toward his people. When a supplier failed to complete a "hot" order on time and Michael's team had to resort to air shipping to meet the customer's deadline, he realized that the profit margin on the sale would be blown. In irritation, he lashed out at his subordinates, demeaning the solid work they had done and disregarding their own frustration with the supplier. In his diary, he admitted as much:

> As of Friday, we have spent $28,000 in air freight to send 1,500 $30 spray jet mops to our number two customer. Another 2,800 remain on this order, and there is a good probability that they too will gain wings. I have turned from the kindly Supply Chain Manager into the black-masked executioner. All similarity to civility is gone, our backs are against the wall, flight is not possible, therefore fight is probable.

Even when managers don't have their backs against the wall, developing long-term strategy and launching new initiatives can often seem more important—and perhaps sexier—than making sure that subordinates have what they need to make steady progress and feel supported as human beings. But as we saw repeatedly in our research, even the best strategy will fail if managers ignore the people working in the trenches to execute it.

A Model Manager—and a Tool for Emulating Him

We could explain the many (and largely unsurprising) moves that can catalyze progress and nourish spirits, but it may be more useful to give an example of a manager who consistently used those moves—and then to provide a simple tool that can help any manager do so.

Our model manager is Graham, whom we observed leading a small team of chemical engineers within a multinational European firm we'll call Kruger-Bern. The mission of the team's NewPoly project was clear and meaningful enough: develop a safe, biodegradable polymer to replace petrochemicals in cosmetics and, eventually, in a wide range of consumer products. As in many large firms, however, the project was nested in a confusing and sometimes threatening corporate setting of shifting top-management priorities, conflicting signals, and wavering commitments. Resources were uncomfortably tight, and uncertainty loomed over the project's future—and every team member's career. Even worse, an incident early in the project, in which an important customer reacted angrily to a sample, left the team reeling. Yet Graham was able to sustain team members' inner work lives by repeatedly and visibly removing obstacles, materially supporting progress, and emotionally supporting the team.

Graham's management approach excelled in four ways. First, he established a positive climate, one event at a time, which set behavioral norms for the entire team. When the customer complaint stopped the project in its tracks, for example, he engaged immediately with the team to analyze the problem, without recriminations, and develop a plan for repairing the relationship. In doing so, he modeled how to respond to crises in the work: not by panicking or pointing fingers but by identifying problems and their causes, and developing a coordinated action plan. This is both a practical approach and a great way to give subordinates a sense of forward movement even in the face of the missteps and failures inherent in any complex project.

Second, Graham stayed attuned to his team's everyday activities and progress. In fact, the nonjudgmental climate he had established made this happen naturally. Team members updated him frequently—without being asked—on their setbacks, progress, and plans. At one point, one of his hardest-working colleagues, Brady, had to abort a trial of a new material because he couldn't get the parameters right on the equipment. It was bad news, because the NewPoly team had access to the equipment only one day a week, but Brady immediately informed Graham. In his diary entry that evening, Brady noted, "He didn't like the lost week but seemed to understand." That understanding assured Graham's place in the stream of information that would allow him to give his people just what they needed to make progress.

Third, Graham targeted his support according to recent events in the team and the project. Each day, he could anticipate what type of intervention—a catalyst or the removal of an inhibitor; a nourisher or some antidote to a toxin—would have the most impact on team members' inner work lives and progress. And if he could not make that judgment, he asked. Most days it was not hard to figure out, as on the day he received some uplifting news about his bosses' commitment to the project. He knew the team was jittery about a rumored corporate reorganization and could use the encouragement. Even though the clarification came during a well-earned vacation day, he immediately got on the phone to relay the good news to the team.

Finally, Graham established himself as a resource for team members, rather than a micromanager; he was sure to *check in* while never seeming to *check up* on them. Superficially, checking in and checking up seem quite similar, but micromanagers make four kinds of mistakes. First, they fail to allow autonomy in carrying out the work. Unlike Graham, who gave the NewPoly team a clear strategic goal but respected members' ideas about how to meet it, micromanagers dictate every move. Second, they frequently ask subordinates about their work without providing any real help. By contrast, when one of Graham's team members reported problems, Graham helped analyze them—remaining open to alternative interpretations—and often ended up helping to get things back on track. Third, micromanagers are quick to affix personal blame when problems arise, leading subordinates to hide problems rather than honestly discuss how to surmount them, as Graham did with Brady. And fourth, micromanagers tend to hoard information to use as a secret weapon. Few realize how damaging this is to inner work life. When subordinates perceive that a manager is withholding potentially useful information, they feel infantilized, their motivation wanes, and their work is handicapped. Graham was quick to communicate upper management's views of the project, customers' opinions and needs, and possible sources of assistance or resistance within and outside the organization.

In all those ways, Graham sustained his team's positive emotions, intrinsic motivation, and favorable perceptions. His actions serve as a powerful example of how managers at any level can approach each day determined to foster progress.

We know that many managers, however well-intentioned, will find it hard to establish the habits that seemed to come so naturally to Graham. Awareness, of course, is the first step. However, turning an awareness of the importance of inner work life into routine action takes discipline. With that in mind, we developed a checklist for managers to consult on a daily basis (see the sidebar "The Daily

The Daily Progress Checklist

NEAR THE END OF EACH WORKDAY, use this checklist to review the day and plan your managerial actions for the next day. After a few days, you will be able to identify issues by scanning the boldface words. First, focus on progress and setbacks and think about specific events (catalysts, nourishers, inhibitors, and toxins) that contributed to them. Next, consider any clear inner-work-life clues and what further information they provide about progress and other events. Finally, prioritize for action. The action plan for the next day is the most important part of your daily review: What is the one thing you can do to best facilitate progress?

Progress

Which 1 or 2 events today indicated either a small win or a possible breakthrough? (Describe briefly.)

Setbacks

Which 1 or 2 events today indicated either a small setback or a possible crisis? (Describe briefly.)

Catalysts

- ☐ Did the team have clear short- and long-term **goals** for meaningful work?

- ☐ Did team members have sufficient **autonomy** to solve problems and take ownership of the project?

- ☐ Did they have all the **resources** they needed to move forward efficiently?

- ☐ Did they have sufficient **time** to focus on meaningful work?

- ☐ Did I give or get them **help** when they needed or requested it? Did I encourage team members to help one another?

- ☐ Did I discuss **lessons** from today's successes and problems with my team?

- ☐ Did I help **ideas** flow freely within the group?

Inhibitors

- ☐ Was there any confusion regarding long- or short-term **goals** for meaningful work?

- ☐ Were team members overly **constrained** in their ability to solve problems and feel ownership of the project?

- ☐ Did they lack any of the **resources** they needed to move forward effectively?

- ☐ Did they lack sufficient **time** to focus on meaningful work?

- ☐ Did I or others fail to provide needed or requested **help**?

- ☐ Did I "punish" failure or neglect to find **lessons** and/ or opportunities in problems and successes?

- ☐ Did I or others cut off the presentation or debate of **ideas** prematurely?

Nourishers

☐ Did I show **respect** to team members by recognizing their contributions to progress, attending to their ideas, and treating them as trusted professionals?

☐ Did I **encourage** team members who faced difficult challenges?

☐ Did I **support** team members who had a personal or professional problem?

☐ Is there a sense of personal and professional **affiliation** and camaraderie within the team?

Toxins

☐ Did I **disrespect** any team members by failing to recognize their contributions to progress, not attending to their ideas, or not treating them as trusted professionals?

☐ Did I **discourage** a member of the team in any way?

☐ Did I **neglect** a team member who had a personal or professional problem?

☐ Is there tension or **antagonism** among members of the team or between team members and me?

Inner work life

Did I see any indications of the quality of my subordinates' inner work lives today?

Perceptions of the work, team, management, firm _____

Emotions _____

Motivation _____

What specific events might have affected inner work life today? _____

Action plan

What can I do tomorrow to strengthen the catalysts and nourishers identified and provide the ones that are lacking?

What can I do tomorrow to start eliminating the inhibitors and toxins identified?

_____

_____

_____

_____

Progress Checklist"). The aim of the checklist is managing for meaningful progress, one day at a time.

The Progress Loop

Inner work life drives performance; in turn, good performance, which depends on consistent progress, enhances inner work life. We call this the *progress loop*; it reveals the potential for self-reinforcing benefits.

So, the most important implication of the progress principle is this: By supporting people and their daily progress in meaningful work, managers improve not only the inner work lives of their employees but also the organization's long-term performance, which enhances inner work life even more. Of course, there is a dark side—the possibility of negative feedback loops. If managers fail to support progress and the people trying to make it, inner work life suffers and so does performance; and degraded performance further undermines inner work life.

A second implication of the progress principle is that managers needn't fret about trying to read the psyches of their workers, or manipulate complicated incentive schemes, to ensure that employees are motivated and happy. As long as they show basic respect and consideration, they can focus on supporting the work itself.

To become an effective manager, you must learn to set this positive feedback loop in motion. That may require a significant shift. Business schools, business books, and managers themselves usually focus on managing organizations or people. But if you focus on managing progress, the management of people—and even of entire organizations—becomes much more feasible. You won't have to figure out how to x-ray the inner work lives of subordinates; if you facilitate their steady progress in meaningful work, make that progress salient to them, and treat them well, they will experience the emotions, motivations, and perceptions necessary for great performance. Their superior work will contribute to organizational success. And here's the beauty of it: They will love their jobs.

Originally published in May 2011. Reprint R1105C

The Price of Incivility

by Christine Porath and Christine Pearson

RUDENESS AT WORK IS RAMPANT, and it's on the rise. Over the past 14 years we've polled thousands of workers about how they're treated on the job, and 98% have reported experiencing uncivil behavior. In 2011 half said they were treated rudely at least once a week—up from a quarter in 1998.

The costs chip away at the bottom line. Nearly everybody who experiences workplace incivility responds in a negative way, in some cases overtly retaliating. Employees are less creative when they feel disrespected, and many get fed up and leave. About half deliberately decrease their effort or lower the quality of their work. And incivility damages customer relationships. Our research shows that people are less likely to buy from a company with an employee they perceive as rude, whether the rudeness is directed at them or at other employees. Witnessing just a single unpleasant interaction leads customers to generalize about other employees, the organization, and even the brand.

We've interviewed employees, managers, HR executives, presidents, and CEOs. We've administered questionnaires, run experiments, led workshops, and spoken with doctors, lawyers, judges, law enforcement officers, architects, engineers, consultants, and coaches about how they've faced and handled incivility. And we've collected data from more than 14,000 people throughout the United

States and Canada in order to track the prevalence, types, causes, costs, and cures of incivility at work. We know two things for certain: Incivility is expensive, and few organizations recognize or take action to curtail it.

In this article we'll discuss our findings, detail the costs, and propose some interventions. But first, let's look at the various shapes incivility can take.

Forms of Incivility

We've all heard of (or experienced) the "boss from hell." The stress of ongoing hostility from a manager takes a toll, sometimes a big one. We spoke with a man we'll call Matt, who reported to Larry—a volatile bully who insulted his direct reports, belittled their efforts, and blamed them for things over which they had no control. (The names in this article have been changed and the identities disguised.) Larry was rude to customers, too. When he accompanied Matt to one client's store, he told the owner, "I see you're carrying on your father's tradition. This store looked like sh-- then. And it looks like sh-- in your hands."

Matt's stress level skyrocketed. He took a risk and reported Larry to HR. (He wasn't the first to complain.) Called on the carpet, Larry failed to apologize, saying only that perhaps he "used an atomic bomb" when he "could have used a flyswatter." Weeks later Larry was named district manager of the year. Three days after that, Matt had a heart attack.

The conclusion of Matt's story is unusual, but unchecked rudeness is surprisingly common. We heard of one boss who was so routinely abusive that employees and suppliers had a code for alerting one another to his impending arrival ("The eagle has landed!"). The only positive aspect was that their shared dislike helped the employees forge close bonds. After the company died, in the late 1990s, its alums formed a network that thrives to this day.

In some cases an entire department is infected. Jennifer worked in an industry that attracted large numbers of educated young professionals willing to work for a pittance in order to be in a creative

Idea in Brief

Leaders can counter rudeness at work both by monitoring their own actions and by fostering civility in others.

Strategies for managing yourself include modeling good behavior and asking for feedback. Turn off your iPhone during meetings, pay attention to questions, and follow up on promises.

When it comes to managing the organization, you should hire for civility, teach it, create group norms, reward positive behavior, penalize rudeness, and seek out former employees for an honest assessment of your company's culture.

Failure to keep tabs on behavior can allow incivility to creep into everyday interactions—and could cost your organization millions in lost employees, lost customers, and lost productivity.

field. It was widely accepted that they had to pay their dues. The atmosphere included door slamming, side conversations, exclusion, and blatant disregard for people's time. Years later Jennifer still cringes as she remembers her boss screaming, "You made a mistake!" when she'd overlooked a minor typo in an internal memo. There was lots of attrition among low-level employees, but those who did stay seemed to absorb the behaviors they'd been subjected to, and they put newcomers through the same kind of abuse.

Fran was a senior executive in a global consumer products company. After several quarters of outstanding growth despite a down economy, she found herself confronted by a newcomer in the C-suite, Joe. For six months Fran had to jump through hoops to defend the business, even though it had defied stagnation. She never got an explanation for why she was picked on, and eventually she left, not for another job but to escape what she called "a soul-destroying experience."

Incivility can take much more subtle forms, and it is often prompted by thoughtlessness rather than actual malice. Think of the manager who sends e-mails during a presentation, or the boss who "teases" direct reports in ways that sting, or the team leader who takes credit for good news but points a finger at team members when something goes wrong. Such relatively minor acts can be even more insidious than overt bullying, because they are less obvious and easier to overlook—yet they add up, eroding engagement and morale.

The Costs of Incivility

Many managers would say that incivility is wrong, but not all recognize that it has tangible costs. Targets of incivility often punish their offenders and the organization, although most hide or bury their feelings and don't necessarily think of their actions as revenge. Through a poll of 800 managers and employees in 17 industries, we learned just how people's reactions play out. Among workers who've been on the receiving end of incivility:

- 48% intentionally decreased their work effort.

- 47% intentionally decreased the time spent at work.

- 38% intentionally decreased the quality of their work.

- 80% lost work time worrying about the incident.

- 63% lost work time avoiding the offender.

- 66% said that their performance declined.

- 78% said that their commitment to the organization declined.

- 12% said that they left their job because of the uncivil treatment.

- 25% admitted to taking their frustration out on customers.

Experiments and other reports offer additional insights about the effects of incivility. Here are some examples of what can happen.

Creativity suffers

In an experiment we conducted with Amir Erez, a professor of management at the University of Florida, participants who were treated rudely by other subjects were 30% less creative than others in the study. They produced 25% fewer ideas, and the ones they did come up with were less original. For example, when asked what to do with a brick, participants who had been treated badly proposed logical but not particularly imaginative activities, such as "build a house," "build a wall," and "build a school." We saw more sparks from participants who had been treated civilly; their suggestions included "sell the brick on eBay," "use it as a goalpost for a street soccer game," "hang it on a museum wall and call it abstract art," and "decorate it like a pet and give it to a kid as a present."

Performance and team spirit deteriorate

Survey results and interviews indicate that simply witnessing incivility has negative consequences. In one experiment we conducted, people who'd observed poor behavior performed 20% worse on word puzzles than other people did. We also found that witnesses to incivility were less likely than others to help out, even when the person they'd be helping had no apparent connection to the uncivil person: Only 25% of the subjects who'd witnessed incivility volunteered to help, whereas 51% of those who hadn't witnessed it did.

Customers turn away

Public rudeness among employees is common, according to our survey of 244 consumers. Whether it's waiters berating fellow waiters or store clerks criticizing colleagues, disrespectful behavior makes people uncomfortable, and they're quick to walk out without making a purchase.

We studied this phenomenon with the USC marketing professors Debbie MacInnis and Valerie Folkes. In one experiment, half the participants witnessed a supposed bank representative publicly reprimanding another for incorrectly presenting credit card information. Only 20% of those who'd seen the encounter said that they would use the bank's services in the future, compared with 80% of those who hadn't. And nearly two-thirds of those who'd seen the exchange said that they would feel anxious dealing with *any* employee of the bank.

What's more, when we tested various scenarios, we found that it didn't matter whether the targeted employee was incompetent, whether the reprimand had been delivered behind closed doors (but overheard), or whether the employee had done something questionable or illegal, such as park in a handicapped spot. Regardless of the circumstances, people don't like to see others treated badly.

Managing incidents is expensive

HR professionals say that just one incident can soak up weeks of attention and effort. According to a study conducted by Accountemps and reported in *Fortune*, managers and executives at *Fortune* 1,000 firms spend 13% of their work time—the equivalent of seven weeks a year—mending employee relationships and otherwise dealing with the aftermath of incivility. And costs soar, of course, when consultants or attorneys must be brought in to help settle a situation.

What's a Leader to Do?

It can take constant vigilance to keep the workplace civil; otherwise, rudeness tends to creep into everyday interactions. Managers can use several strategies to keep their own behavior in check and to foster civility among others.

Managing yourself

Leaders set the tone, so you need to be aware of your actions and of how you come across to others.

Model good behavior. In one of our surveys, 25% of managers who admitted to having behaved badly said they were uncivil because their leaders—their own role models—were rude. If employees see that those who have climbed the corporate ladder tolerate or embrace uncivil behavior, they're likely to follow suit. So turn off your iPhone during meetings, pay attention to questions, and follow up on promises.

One way to help create a culture of respect and bring out your employees' best is to express your appreciation. Personal notes are particularly effective, especially if they emphasize being a role model, treating people well, and living the organization's values. Doug Conant, a former CEO of Campbell Soup, is well aware of the power of personal recognition. During his tenure as president and CEO, he sent more than 30,000 handwritten notes of thanks to employees.

Ask for feedback. You may need a reality check from the people who work for you. A manager at Hanover Insurance decided to ask his employees what they liked and didn't like about his leadership style. He learned that it really bothered them when he glanced at his phone or responded to e-mail during meetings. He now refrains from those activities, and his team appreciates the change.

Employees won't always be honest, but there are tools you can use on your own. For example, keep a journal in which you track instances of civility and incivility and note changes that you'd like to make.

Pay attention to your progress. As Josef, an IT professional, learned more about incivility, he became aware of his tendency to disparage a few nasty colleagues behind their backs. "I hadn't thought about it much until I considered the negative role modeling I was doing," he told us. "I criticized only people who were obnoxious to others and shared my criticisms only with people I trusted and in private, and somehow that made it seem OK. Then I started thinking about how I was just adding to the divide by spreading gossip and creating 'sides.' It was a real eye-opener, and I decided that I wanted to set a better example."

Within a short time Josef noticed that he was logging fewer occasions when he gossiped negatively and that he felt better about himself and his workplace. "I don't know whether anyone else would notice a difference—people already thought I was fair and supportive—but I know that I've changed," he said. "And there's another benefit for all of us: I'm seeing less incivility around me. I think that speaking up when colleagues or subordinates are rude can really make a difference. It puts them on alert that somebody is watching and cares how everyone is treated."

Managing the organization

Monitoring and adjusting your own behavior is an important piece of the puzzle, but you need to take action across the company as well.

Hire for civility. Avoid bringing incivility into the workplace to begin with. Some companies, including Southwest Airlines and Four Seasons, put civility at the fore when they interview applicants.

It's useful to give your team members a say about their prospective colleagues; they may pick up on behavior that would be suppressed in more-formal interviews. Rhapsody, an online subscription music service, conducts group interviews so that employees can evaluate potential teammates. It has been known to turn down applicants who are strong on paper but make the team uncomfortable in some way. In one case, a team considering two applicants felt that the apparently stronger one lacked emotional intelligence: She talked too much and seemed unwilling to listen. So the company hired the other candidate, who has worked out very well.

Only 11% of organizations report considering civility at all during the hiring process, and many of those investigate it in a cursory fashion. But incivility usually leaves a trail of some sort, which can be uncovered if someone's willing to look. One hospital had a near miss when bringing on a new radiologist. It offered the job to Dirk, a talented doctor who came highly recommended by his peers and had aced the interviews. But one assistant in the department had a hunch that something was off. Through a network of personal contacts, she learned that Dirk had left a number of badly treated subordinates in his wake—information that would never have surfaced from his CV. So the department head nixed the hire, telling Dirk that if he accepted the offer, the hospital would let him go right away, which would raise a flag for potential employers.

Teach civility. We're always amazed by how many managers and employees tell us that they don't understand what it means to be civil. One quarter of the offenders we surveyed said that they didn't recognize their behavior as uncivil.

People can learn civility on the job. Role-playing is one technique. At one hospital in Los Angeles, temperamental doctors have to attend "charm school" to decrease their brashness (and reduce the potential for lawsuits). Some organizations offer classes on managing the generation mix, in which they talk about differences in norms of civility and how to improve behavior across generations.

Video can be a good teaching tool, especially when paired with coaching. Film employees during various interactions so that they can observe their own facial expressions, posture, words, and tone of voice. It takes people a while to learn to ignore the camera, but eventually they resume their normal patterns of behavior.

After participating in such an exercise, the CEO of a medical firm told us, "I didn't realize what a jerk I sounded like." To his credit, he used the insight to fashion more-civil communication—and became less of a jerk. Another senior executive reported that he'd always thought he maintained a poker face, but the video revealed obvious "tells." For instance, if he lost interest in a discussion, he'd look away.

We recommend that after being taped, people watch the video in three modes: first, with both sound and image, to get an overall sense of their demeanor; second, without sound, to focus on nonverbal behaviors such as gestures, distancing, and facial expressions; and third, with only sound, to highlight tone of voice, volume and speed of speech, and word choice. People don't take issue just with words; tone can be equally or more potent.

Create group norms. Start a dialogue with your team about expectations. An insurance executive told us that he'd talked with his team about what behaviors worked and what didn't. By the end of the first meeting, the team had produced and taken ownership of concrete norms for civility, such as arriving on time and ignoring e-mail during meetings.

In one of our own workplaces, we've borrowed a practice from sports to take the edge off and to help one another avoid falling into occasional abrasiveness. In our world, incivility can flare up during presentations, because overly zealous professors may vigorously interrogate colleagues and visiting professors in an effort to demonstrate their own intellect. We warn colleagues who are engaging in this behavior by using hand signals to indicate the equivalent of soccer's yellow and red cards. The "yellow card" sign (a fist raised to the side of the head) conveys a warning, letting the interrogator know she needs to think about the phrasing, tone, and intensity of her comments and questions. The "red card" signal (two fingers held up, followed by the classic heave of the thumb) means she's finished for the session—she's been so offensive, repeatedly and after fair warning, that she needs to be "ejected from the game." Faculty members have learned that when they get the red card signal, they have to button it—no more today.

Ochsner Health System, a large Louisiana health care provider, has adopted what it calls "the 10/5 way": If you're within 10 feet of someone, make eye contact and smile. If you're within five feet, say hello. Ochsner has seen greater patient satisfaction and an increase in patient referrals as a result.

Reward good behavior. Collegiality should be a consideration in every performance review, but many companies think only about outcomes and tend to overlook damaging behaviors. What behavior does your review system motivate? All too often we see organizations badly miss the mark. They want collaboration, but you'd never know it from their evaluation forms, which focus entirely on individual assessment, without a single measure of teamwork.

Zappos implemented a "Wow" recognition program designed to capture people in the act of doing the right thing. Any employee at any level who sees a colleague doing something special can award a "Wow," which includes a cash bonus of up to $50. Recipients are automatically eligible for a "Hero" award. Heroes are chosen by top executives; they receive a covered parking spot for a month, a $150 Zappos gift card, and, with full symbolic flair, a hero's cape. Even lighthearted awards like these can be powerful symbols of the importance of civility.

Penalize bad behavior. Even the best companies occasionally make bad hires, and employees from an acquired firm may be accustomed to different norms. The trick is to identify and try to correct any troublesome behavior. Companies often avoid taking action, though, and most incidents go unreported, partly because employees know nothing will come of a report. If you want to foster respect, take complaints seriously and follow up.

Rather than confronting offenders, leaders often opt for an easier solution—moving them to a different location. The result is predictable: The behavior continues in a new setting. One manager told us that his department has been burned so often that it no longer considers internal candidates for managerial positions.

Sometimes the best path is to let someone go. Danny Meyer, the owner of many successful restaurants in Manhattan, will fire talent for uncivil behavior. Gifted but rude chefs don't last at his restaurants because they set off bad vibes. Meyer believes that customers can *taste* employee incivility, even when the behavior occurs in the kitchen.

Many top law firms, hospitals, and businesses we've dealt with have learned the hard way that it simply doesn't pay to harbor habitual offenders, even if they're rainmakers or protégés. Whether offenders have caused multimillion-dollar lawsuits or been responsible for the exit of throngs of employees, often the losses could have been mitigated by early, resolute action. A senior executive of a highly successful company told us recently, "Every mistake we've made in firing a questionable hire was in taking action too late, not too early."

Conduct postdeparture interviews. Organizational memory fades quickly. It's crucial, therefore, to gather information from and reflect on the experiences and reactions of employees who leave because of incivility. If you ask targets during their exit interviews why they're leaving, you'll usually get only vague responses. Interviews conducted six months or so later can yield a truer picture. Talking with former employees after they've distanced themselves from the organization and settled into their new work environments can give you insights about the violations of civility that prompted them to leave.

Companies we've worked with calculate that the tab for incivility can run into the millions. Some years back Cisco put together a detailed estimate of what incivility was costing the company. It factored in its reputation as a consistently great place to work, assumed an extremely low probability of rudeness among its employees, and looked at only three potential costs. Even in this exemplary workplace, it was estimated that incivility cost $12 million a year. That realization led to the creation of Cisco's global workplace civility program.

We close with a warning to those who think consistent civility is an extravagance: Just one habitually offensive employee critically positioned in your organization can cost you dearly in lost employees, lost customers, and lost productivity.

Originally published in January–February 2013. Reprint R1301J

What Most People Get Wrong About Men and Women

by Catherine H. Tinsley and Robin J. Ely

THE CONVERSATION ABOUT the treatment of women in the workplace has reached a crescendo of late, and senior leaders—men as well as women—are increasingly vocal about a commitment to gender parity. That's all well and good, but there's an important catch. The discussions, and many of the initiatives companies have undertaken, too often reflect a faulty belief: that men and women are fundamentally *different*, by virtue of their genes or their upbringing or both. Of course, there are biological differences. But those are not the differences people are usually talking about. Instead, the rhetoric focuses on the idea that women are inherently unlike men in terms of disposition, attitudes, and behaviors. (Think headlines that tout "Why women do X at the office" or "Working women don't Y.")

One set of assumed differences is marshaled to explain women's failure to achieve parity with men: Women negotiate poorly, lack confidence, are too risk-averse, or don't put in the requisite hours at work because they value family more than their careers. Simultaneously, other assumed differences—that women are more caring, cooperative, or mission-driven—are used as a rationale for companies to invest in women's success. But whether framed as a barrier or a benefit, these beliefs hold women back. We will not level the playing field so long as the bedrock on which it rests is our conviction about how the sexes are different.

The reason is simple: Science, by and large, does not actually support these claims. There is wide variation among women and among men, and meta-analyses show that, on average, the sexes are far more similar in their inclinations, attitudes, and skills than popular opinion would have us believe. We do see sex differences in various settings, including the workplace—but those differences are not rooted in fixed gender traits. Rather, they stem from organizational structures, company practices, and patterns of interaction that position men and women differently, creating systematically different experiences for them. When facing dissimilar circumstances, people respond differently—not because of their sex but because of their situations.

Emphasizing sex differences runs the risk of making them seem natural and inevitable. As anecdotes that align with stereotypes are told and retold, without addressing why and when stereotypical behaviors appear, sex differences are exaggerated and take on a determinative quality. Well-meaning but largely ineffectual interventions then focus on "fixing" women or accommodating them rather than on changing the circumstances that gave rise to different behaviors in the first place.

Take, for example, the common belief that women are more committed to family than men are. Research simply does not support that notion. In a study of Harvard Business School graduates that one of us conducted, nearly everyone, regardless of gender, placed a higher value on their families than on their work (see "Rethink What You 'Know' About High-Achieving Women," HBR, December 2014). Moreover, having made career decisions to accommodate family responsibilities didn't explain the gender achievement gap. Other research, too, makes it clear that men and women do not have fundamentally different priorities.

Numerous studies show that what does differ is the treatment mothers and fathers receive when they start a family. Women (but not men) are seen as needing support, whereas men are more likely

Idea in Brief

The Belief

There's a popular notion that men and women are fundamentally different in important (nonbiological) ways—and those differences are cited to explain women's lagged achievement.

The Truth

According to numerous meta-analyses of published research, men and women are actually very similar with respect to key attri-

butes such as confidence, appetite for risk, and negotiating skill.

Why It Matters

Too many managers try to "fix" women or accommodate their supposed differences—and that doesn't work. Companies must instead address the organizational conditions that lead to lower rates of retention and promotion for women.

to get the message—either explicit or subtle—that they need to "man up" and not voice stress and fatigue. If men do ask, say, for a lighter travel schedule, their supervisors may cut them some slack—but often grudgingly and with the clear expectation that the reprieve is temporary. Accordingly, some men attempt an under-the-radar approach, quietly reducing hours or travel and hoping it goes unnoticed, while others simply concede, limiting the time they spend on family responsibilities and doubling down at work. Either way, they maintain a reputation that keeps them on an upward trajectory. Meanwhile, mothers are often expected, indeed encouraged, to ratchet back at work. They are rerouted into less taxing roles and given less "demanding" (read: lower-status, less career-enhancing) clients.

To sum up, men's and women's desires and challenges about work/family balance are remarkably similar. It is what they experience at work once they become parents that puts them in very different places.

Things don't have to be this way. When companies observe differences in the overall success rates of women and men, or in behaviors that are critical to effectiveness, they can actively seek to understand the organizational conditions that might be responsible, and then they can experiment with changing those conditions.

Consider the example of a savvy managing director concerned about the leaky pipeline at her professional services firm. Skeptical that women were simply "opting out" following the birth of a child, she investigated and found that one reason women were leaving the firm stemmed from the performance appraisal system: Supervisors had to adhere to a forced distribution when rating their direct reports, and women who had taken parental leave were unlikely to receive the highest rating because their performance was ranked against that of peers who had worked a full year. Getting less than top marks not only hurt their chances of promotion but also sent a demoralizing message that being a mother was incompatible with being on a partner track. However, the fix was relatively easy: The company decided to reserve the forced distribution for employees who worked the full year, while those with long leaves could roll over their rating from the prior year. That applied to both men and women, but the policy was most heavily used by new mothers. The change gave women more incentive to return from maternity leave and helped keep them on track for advancement. Having more mothers stay on track, in turn, helped chip away at assumptions within the firm about women's work/family preferences.

As this example reveals, companies need to dive deeper into their beliefs, norms, practices, and policies to understand how they position women relative to men and how the different positions fuel inequality. Seriously investigating the context that gives rise to differential patterns in the way men and women experience the workplace—and intervening accordingly—can help companies chart a path to gender parity.

Below, we address three popular myths about how the sexes differ and explain how each manifests itself in organizational discourse about women's lagged advancement. Drawing on years of social science research, we debunk the myths and offer alternative explanations for observed sex differences—explanations that point to ways that managers can level the playing field. We then offer a four-pronged strategy for undertaking such actions.

Popular Myths

We've all heard statements in the media and in companies that women lack *the desire or ability to negotiate,* that they lack *confidence,* and that they lack *an appetite for risk.* And, the thinking goes, those shortcomings explain why women have so far failed to reach parity with men.

For decades, studies have examined sex differences on these three dimensions, enabling social scientists to conduct meta-analyses—investigations that reveal whether or not, on average across studies, sex differences hold, and if so, how large the differences are. (See the sidebar "The Power of Meta-Analysis.") Just as importantly, meta-analyses also reveal the circumstances under which differences between men and women are more or less likely to arise. The aggregated findings are clear: Context explains any sex differences that exist in the workplace.

Take negotiation. Over and over, we hear that women are poor negotiators—they "settle too easily," are "too nice," or are "too cooperative." But not so, according to research. Jens Mazei and colleagues recently analyzed more than 100 studies examining whether men and women negotiate different outcomes; they determined that gender differences were small to negligible. Men have a slight advantage in negotiations when they are advocating exclusively for themselves and when ambiguity about the stakes or opportunities is high. Larger disparities in outcomes occur when negotiators either have no prior experience or are forced to negotiate, as in a mandated training exercise. But such situations are atypical, and even when they do arise, statisticians would deem the resulting sex differences to be small. As for the notion that women are more cooperative than men, research by Daniel Balliet and colleagues refutes that.

The belief that women lack confidence is another fallacy. That assertion is commonly invoked to explain why women speak up less in meetings and do not put themselves forward for promotions unless they are 100% certain they meet all the job requirements. But research does not corroborate the idea that women are less confident than men. Analyzing more than 200 studies, Kristen Kling and colleagues concluded that the only noticeable differences occurred during adolescence; starting at age 23, differences become negligible.

What about risk taking—are women really more conservative than men? Many people believe that's true—though they are split on whether being risk-averse is a strength or a weakness. On the positive side, the thinking goes, women are less likely to get caught up in macho displays of bluff and bravado and thus are less likely to take unnecessary risks. Consider the oft-heard sentiment following the demise of Lehman Brothers: "If Lehman Brothers had been Lehman Sisters, the financial crisis might have been averted." On the negative side, women are judged as too cautious to make high-risk, potentially high-payoff investments.

But once again, research fails to support either of these stereotypes. As with negotiation, sex differences in the propensity to take risks are small and depend on the context. In a meta-analysis performed by James Byrnes and colleagues, the largest differences arise in contexts unlikely to exist in most organizations (such as among people asked to participate in a game of pure chance). Similarly, in a study Peggy Dwyer and colleagues ran examining the largest, last, and riskiest investments made by nearly 2,000 mutual fund investors, sex differences were very small. More importantly, when investors' specific knowledge about the investments was added to the equation, the sex difference diminished to near extinction, suggesting that access to information, not propensity for risk taking, explains the small sex differences that have been documented.

In short, a wealth of evidence contradicts each of these popular myths. Yet they live on through oft-repeated narratives routinely invoked to explain women's lagged advancement.

More-Plausible Explanations

The extent to which employees are able to thrive and succeed at work depends partly on the kinds of opportunities and treatment they receive. People are more likely to behave in ways that undermine their chances for success when they are disconnected from information networks, when they are judged or penalized dispropor-

Why the Sex-Difference Narrative Persists

BELIEFS IN SEX DIFFERENCES have staying power partly because they uphold conventional gender norms, preserve the gender status quo, and require no upheaval of existing organizational practices or work arrangements. But they are also the path of least resistance for our brains. Three well-documented cognitive errors help explain the endurance of the sex-difference narrative.

First, when seeking to explain others' behavior, we gravitate to explanations based on intrinsic *personality traits*—including stereotypically "male" traits and stereotypically "female" traits—rather than *contextual factors*. (Social psychologists call this "the fundamental attribution error.") For example, if a man speaks often and forcefully in a meeting, we are more likely to conclude that he is assertive and confident than to search for a situational explanation, such as that he's been repeatedly praised for his contributions. Likewise, if a woman is quiet in a meeting, the easier explanation is that she's meek or underconfident; it takes more cognitive energy to construct an alternative account, such as that she is used to being cut off or ignored when she speaks. In short, when we see men and women behaving in gender-stereotypical ways, we tend to make the most cognitively simple assumption—that the behavior reflects who they are rather than the situation they are in.

Second, mere exposure to a continuing refrain, such as "Women are X, and men are Y," makes people judge the statement as true. Many beliefs—that bats are blind, that fresh produce is always more nutritious than frozen, that you shouldn't wake a sleepwalker—are repeated so often that their mere familiarity makes them easier for our minds to accept as truth. (This is called the "mere exposure effect.")

Third, once people believe something is true, they tend to seek, notice, and remember evidence that confirms the position and to ignore or forget evidence that would challenge it. (Psychologists call this "confirmation bias.") If we believe that gender stereotypes are accurate, we are more likely to expect, notice, and remember times when men and women behave in gender-stereotypical ways and to overlook times when they don't.

---

tionately harshly for mistakes or failures, and when they lack feedback. Unfortunately, women are more likely than men to encounter each of these situations. And the way they respond—whether that's by failing to drive a hard bargain, to speak up, or to take risks—gets unfairly attributed to "the way women are," when in fact the culprit is very likely the differential conditions they face.

Multiple studies show, for example, that women are less embedded in networks that offer opportunities to gather vital information and garner support. When people lack access to useful contacts and information, they face a disadvantage in negotiations. They may not know what is on the table, what is within the realm of possibility, or even that a chance to strike a deal exists. When operating under such conditions, women are more likely to conform to the gender stereotype that "women don't ask."

We saw this dynamic vividly play out when comparing the experiences of two professionals we'll call Mary and Rick. (In this example and others that follow, we have changed the names and some details to maintain confidentiality.) Mary and Rick were both midlevel advisers in the wealth management division of a financial services firm. Rick was able to bring in more assets to manage because he sat on the board of a nonprofit, giving him access to a pool of potential clients with high net worth. What Mary did not know for many years is how Rick had gained that advantage. Through casual conversations with one of the firm's senior partners, with whom he regularly played tennis, Rick had learned that discretionary funds existed to help advisers cultivate relationships with clients. So he arranged for the firm to make a donation to the nonprofit. He then began attending the nonprofit's fundraising events and hobnobbing with key players, eventually parlaying his connections into a seat on the board. Mary, by contrast, had no informal relationships with senior partners at the firm and no knowledge of the level of resources that could have helped her land clients.

When people are less embedded, they are also less aware of opportunities for stretch assignments and promotions, and their supervisors may be in the dark about their ambitions. But when women fail to "lean in" and seek growth opportunities, it is easy to assume that they lack the confidence to do so—not that they lack pertinent information. Julie's experience is illustrative. Currently the CEO of a major investment fund, Julie had left her previous employer of 15 years after learning that a more junior male colleague had leapfrogged over her to fill an opening she didn't even know existed. When she announced that she was leaving and why, her boss was surprised. He told her that if he had realized she wanted to move up, he would have gladly helped position her for the promotion. But because she hadn't put her hat in the ring, he had assumed she lacked confidence in her ability to handle the job.

How people react to someone's mistake or failure can also affect that person's ability to thrive and succeed. Several studies have found that because women operate under a higher-resolution microscope than their male counterparts do, their mistakes and failures are scrutinized more carefully and punished more severely. People who are scrutinized more carefully will, in turn, be less likely to speak up in meetings, particularly if they feel no one has their back. However, when women fail to speak up, it is commonly assumed that they lack confidence in their ideas.

We saw a classic example of this dynamic at a biotech company in which team leaders noticed that their female colleagues, all highly qualified research scientists, participated far less in team meetings than their male counterparts did, yet later, in one-on-one conversations, often offered insightful ideas germane to the discussion. What these leaders had failed to see was that when women did speak in meetings, their ideas tended to be either ignored until a man restated them or shot down quickly if they contained even the slightest flaw. In contrast, when men's ideas were flawed, the meritorious elements were salvaged. Women therefore felt they needed to be 110% sure of their ideas before they would venture to share them. In a context in which being smart was the coin of the realm, it seemed better to remain silent than to have one's ideas repeatedly dismissed.

It stands to reason that people whose missteps are more likely to be held against them will also be less likely to take risks. That was the case at a Big Four accounting firm that asked us to investigate why so few women partners were in formal leadership roles. The reason, many believed, was that women did not want such roles because of their family responsibilities, but our survey revealed a more complex story. First, women and men were equally likely to say they would accept a leadership role if offered one, but men were nearly 50% more likely to have been offered one. Second, women were more likely than men to say that worries about jeopardizing their careers deterred them from pursuing leadership positions—they feared they would not recover from failure and thus could not afford to take the risks an effective leader would need to take. Research confirms that such concerns are valid. For example, studies by Victoria Brescoll and colleagues found that if women in male-dominated occupations make mistakes, they are accorded less status and seen as less competent than men making the same mistakes; a study by Ashleigh Rosette and Robert Livingston demonstrated that black women leaders are especially vulnerable to this bias.

Research also shows that women get less frequent and lower-quality feedback than men. When people don't receive feedback, they are less likely to know their worth in negotiations. Moreover, people who receive little feedback are ill-equipped to assess their strengths, shore up their weaknesses, and judge their prospects for success and are therefore less able to build the confidence they need to proactively seek promotions or make risky decisions.

An example of this dynamic comes from a consulting firm in which HR staff members delivered partners' annual feedback to associates. The HR folks noticed that when women were told they were "doing fine," they "freaked out," feeling damned by faint praise; when men received the same feedback, they left the meeting "feeling great." HR concluded that women lack self-confidence and are therefore more sensitive to feedback, so the team advised partners to be especially encouraging to the women associates and to soften any criticism. Many of the partners were none too pleased to have to treat a subset of their associates with kid gloves, grousing that "if women can't stand the heat, they should get out of the kitchen." What these partners failed to realize, however, is that the kitchen was a lot hotter for women in the firm than for men. Why? Because the partners felt more comfortable with the men and so were systematically giving them more informal, day-to-day feedback. When women heard in their annual review that they were doing "fine," it was often the first feedback they'd received all year; they had nothing else to go on and assumed it meant their performance was merely adequate. In contrast, when men heard they were doing "fine," it was but one piece of information amidst a steady stream. The upshot was disproportionate turnover among women associates, many of whom left the firm because they believed their prospects for promotion were slim.

An Alternative Approach

The problem with the sex-difference narrative is that it leads companies to put resources into "fixing" women, which means that women miss out on what they need—and what every employee deserves: a context that enables them to reach their potential and maximizes their chances to succeed.

Managers who are advancing gender equity in their firms are taking a more inquisitive approach—rejecting old scripts, seeking an evidence-based understanding of how women experience the workplace, and then creating the conditions that increase women's prospects for success. Their approach entails four steps:

1. Question the narrative

A consulting firm we worked with had recruited significant numbers of talented women into its entry ranks—and then struggled to promote them. Their supervisors' explanations? Women are insufficiently competitive, lack "fire in the belly," or don't have the requisite confidence to excel in the job. But those narratives did not ring true to Sarah, a regional head, because a handful of women—those within her region—were performing and advancing at par. So rather than accept her colleagues' explanations, she got curious.

2. Generate a plausible alternative explanation

Sarah investigated the factors that might have helped women in her region succeed and found that they received more hands-on training and more attention from supervisors than did women in other regions. This finding suggested that the problem lay not with women's deficiencies but with their differential access to the conditions that enhance self-confidence and success.

To test that hypothesis, Sarah designed an experiment, with our help. First, we randomly split 60 supervisors into two groups of 30 for a training session on coaching junior consultants. Trainers gave both groups the same lecture on how to be a good coach. With one group, however, trainers shared research showing that differences in men's and women's self-confidence are minuscule, thus subtly giving the members of this "treatment" group reason to question gender stereotypes. The "control" group didn't get that information. Next, trainers gave all participants a series of hypotheticals in which an employee—sometimes a man and sometimes a woman—was underperforming. In both groups, participants were asked to write down the feedback they would give the underperforming employee.

Clear differences emerged between the two groups. Supervisors in the control group took different tacks with the underperforming man and woman: They were far less critical of the woman and focused largely on making her feel good, whereas they gave the man feedback that was more direct, specific, and critical, often with concrete suggestions for how he could improve. In contrast, the supervisors who had been shown research that refuted sex differences in self-confidence gave both employees the same kind of feedback; they also asked for more-granular information about the employee's performance so that they could deliver constructive comments. We were struck by how the participants who had been given a reason to question gender stereotypes focused on learning more about individuals' specific performance problems.

The experiment confirmed Sarah's sense that women's lagged advancement might be due at least partly to supervisors' assumptions about the training and development needs of their female direct reports. Moreover, her findings gave supervisors a plausible alternative explanation for women's lagged advancement—a necessary precondition for taking the next step. Although different firms find different types of evidence more or less compelling—not all require as rigorous a test as this firm did—Sarah's evidence-based approach illustrates a key part of the strategy we are advocating.

3. Change the context and assess the results
Once a plausible alternative explanation has been developed, companies can make appropriate changes and see if performance improves. Two stories help illustrate this step. Both come from a

midmarket private equity firm that was trying to address a problem that had persisted for 10 years: The company's promotion and retention rates for white women and people of color were far lower than its hiring rates.

The first story involves Elaine, an Asian-American senior associate who wanted to sharpen her financing skills and asked Dave, a partner, if she could assist with that aspect of his next deal. He invited her to lunch, but when they met, he was underwhelmed. Elaine struck him as insufficiently assertive and overly cautious. He decided against putting her on his team—but then he had second thoughts. The partners had been questioning their ability to spot and develop talent, especially in the case of associates who didn't look like them. Dave thus decided to try an experiment: He invited Elaine to join the team and then made a conscious effort to treat her exactly as he would have treated someone he deemed a superstar. He introduced her to the relevant players in the industry, told the banks she would be leading the financing, and gave her lots of rope but also enough feedback and coaching so that she wouldn't hang herself. Elaine did not disappoint; indeed, her performance was stellar. While quiet in demeanor, Dave's new protégée showed an uncanny ability to read the client and come up with creative approaches to the deal's financing.

A second example involves Ned, a partner who was frustrated that Joan, a recent-MBA hire on his team, didn't assert herself on management team calls. At first Ned simply assumed that Joan lacked confidence. But then it occurred to him that he might be falling back on gender stereotypes, and he took a closer look at his own behavior. He realized that he wasn't doing anything to make participation easier for her and was actually doing things that made it harder, like taking up all the airtime on calls. So they talked about it, and Joan admitted that she was afraid of making a mistake and was hyperaware that if she spoke, she needed to say something very smart. Ned realized that he, too, was afraid she would make a mistake or wouldn't add value to the discussion, which is partly why he took over. But on reflection, he saw that it wouldn't be the end of the world if she did stumble—he did the same himself now and again.

The Power of Meta-Analysis

A META-ANALYSIS is a statistical technique used to combine the results of many studies, providing a more reliable basis for drawing conclusions from research. This approach has three advantages over a single study.

First, it is more *accurate*, because it is based on a very large sample—the total of the samples across all the studies—and because it contains data collected in many different contexts. Any single set of findings may reflect idiosyncrasies of the study's sample or context and thus may not yield conclusions that are truly generalizable. A meta-analysis, in essence, averages across these idiosyncrasies to give us a truer answer to the research question (in this case, "Are men and women different with regard to a particular trait or behavior?").

Second, a meta-analysis is more *comprehensive*. Because it contains studies conducted in many different contexts, it can tell us in which kinds of contexts we are more or less likely to see sex differences.

Third, a meta-analysis is more *precise*: It can tell us just how different men and women are. For any given trait or behavior, there is variability *among* men and *among* women; typically, those within-group differences are distributed around some "true" average for each group. Using the averages and the variability within each group, we can calculate an "effect size" that can be thought of as the impact that sex has on a particular trait. When testing for a sex difference, we are in essence asking the question "How much overlap is there between women and men, or, stated another way, how far apart are their respective averages, relative to the variability within each sex?"

Take the left-hand graph, which shows the distribution of men's and women's heights in the UK. We can see from the curves that men, on average, are quite a bit taller than women. In fact, men average five feet, nine inches, and women five feet, three inches—a six-inch difference. We can also see that a

For their next few calls, they went over the agenda beforehand and worked out which parts she would take the lead on; he then gave her feedback after the call. Ned now has a junior colleague to whom he can delegate more; Joan, meanwhile, feels more confident and has learned that she can take risks and recover from mistakes.

4. Promote continual learning

Both Dave and Ned recognized that their tendency to jump to conclusions based on stereotypes was robbing them—and the firm—of number of women are taller than the average man, just as a number of men are shorter than the average woman. The size of the sex effect on height is 1.72, which is considered "large."

Using that sex difference as a reference point, we can see from the right-hand graph that the difference between men and women in self-esteem, or confidence, is much smaller, with an effect size of 0.10. Although the difference in each graph is statistically significant, the difference in confidence is considered, from a statistical point of view, "trivial"—and from a managerial point of view, essentially meaningless. This same analysis for men's and women's negotiation outcomes and for their propensity to take risks yielded effect sizes of 0.20 ("small") and 0.13 ("trivial"), respectively. In short, contrary to popular belief, all three sex differences we consider in this article are, for all intents and purposes, meaningless.

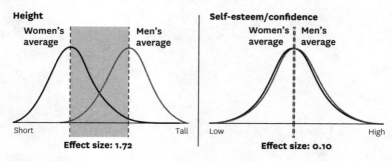

Height
Women's average   Men's average
Short   Tall
Effect size: 1.72

Self-esteem/confidence
Women's average   Men's average
Low   High
Effect size: 0.10

Note: Statisticians consider an effect size of less than 0.20 to be "trivial," 0.20–0.49 to be "small," 0.50–0.79 to be "medium," and 0.80 or more to be "large."

vital talent. Moreover, they have seen firsthand how questioning assumptions and proactively changing conditions gives women the opportunity to develop and shine. The lessons from these small-scale experiments are ongoing: Partners at the firm now meet regularly to discuss what they're learning. They also hold one another accountable for questioning and testing gender-stereotypical assessments as they arise. As a result, old narratives about women's limitations are beginning to give way to new narratives about how the firm can better support all employees.

The four steps we've outlined are consistent with research suggesting that on difficult issues such as gender and race, managers respond more positively when they see themselves as part of the solution rather than simply part of the problem. The solution to women's lagged advancement is not to fix women or their managers but to fix the conditions that undermine women and reinforce gender stereotypes. Furthermore, by taking an inquisitive, evidence-based approach to understanding behavior, companies can not only address gender disparities but also cultivate a learning orientation and a culture that gives all employees the opportunity to reach their full potential.

Originally published in May–June 2018. Reprint R1803J

How Netflix Reinvented HR

by Patty McCord

SHERYL SANDBERG HAS CALLED it one of the most important documents ever to come out of Silicon Valley. It's been viewed more than 5 million times on the web. But when Reed Hastings and I (along with some colleagues) wrote a PowerPoint deck explaining how we shaped the culture and motivated performance at Netflix, where Hastings is CEO and I was chief talent officer from 1998 to 2012, we had no idea it would go viral. We realized that some of the talent management ideas we'd pioneered, such as the concept that workers should be allowed to take whatever vacation time they feel is appropriate, had been seen as a little crazy (at least until other companies started adopting them). But we were surprised that an unadorned set of 127 slides—no music, no animation—would become so influential.

People find the Netflix approach to talent and culture compelling for a few reasons. The most obvious one is that Netflix has been really successful: During 2013 alone its stock more than tripled, it won three Emmy awards, and its US subscriber base grew to nearly 29 million. All that aside, the approach is compelling because it derives from common sense. In this article I'll go beyond the bullet points to describe five ideas that have defined the way Netflix attracts, retains, and manages talent. But first I'll share two conversations I had with early employees, both of which helped shape our overall philosophy.

The first took place in late 2001. Netflix had been growing quickly: We'd reached about 120 employees and had been planning an IPO. But after the dot-com bubble burst and the 9/11 attacks occurred, things changed. It became clear that we needed to put the IPO on hold and lay off a third of our employees. It was brutal. Then, a bit unexpectedly, DVD players became the hot gift that Christmas. By early 2002 our DVD-by-mail subscription business was growing like crazy. Suddenly we had far more work to do, with 30% fewer employees.

One day I was talking with one of our best engineers, an employee I'll call John. Before the layoffs, he'd managed three engineers, but now he was a one-man department working very long hours. I told John I hoped to hire some help for him soon. His response surprised me. "There's no rush—I'm happier now," he said. It turned out that the engineers we'd laid off weren't spectacular—they were merely adequate. John realized that he'd spent too much time riding herd on them and fixing their mistakes. "I've learned that I'd rather work by myself than with subpar performers," he said. His words echo in my mind whenever I describe the most basic element of Netflix's talent philosophy: The best thing you can do for employees—a perk better than foosball or free sushi—is hire only "A" players to work alongside them. Excellent colleagues trump everything else.

The second conversation took place in 2002, a few months after our IPO. Laura, our bookkeeper, was bright, hardworking, and creative. She'd been very important to our early growth, having devised a system for accurately tracking movie rentals so that we could pay the correct royalties. But now, as a public company, we needed CPAs and other fully credentialed, deeply experienced accounting professionals—and Laura had only an associate's degree from a community college. Despite her work ethic, her track record, and the fact that we all really liked her, her skills were no longer adequate. Some of us talked about jury-rigging a new role for her, but we decided that wouldn't be right.

So I sat down with Laura and explained the situation—and said that in light of her spectacular service, we would give her a spectacular severance package. I'd braced myself for tears or histrionics, but

Idea in Brief

The Idea

If a company hires correctly, workers will want to be star performers, and they can be managed through honest communication and common sense. Most companies focus too much on formal policies aimed at the small number of employees whose interests *aren't* fully aligned with the firm's.

The Solution

Hire, reward, and tolerate only fully formed adults. Tell the truth about performance. Make clear to managers that their top priority is building great teams. Leaders should create the company culture, and talent managers should think like innovative businesspeople and not fall into the traditional HR mind-set.

Laura reacted well: She was sad to be leaving but recognized that the generous severance would let her regroup, retrain, and find a new career path. This incident helped us create the other vital element of our talent management philosophy: If we wanted only "A" players on our team, we had to be willing to let go of people whose skills no longer fit, no matter how valuable their contributions had once been. Out of fairness to such people—and, frankly, to help us overcome our discomfort with discharging them—we learned to offer rich severance packages.

With these two overarching principles in mind, we shaped our approach to talent using the five tenets below.

Hire, Reward, and Tolerate Only Fully Formed Adults

Over the years we learned that if we asked people to rely on logic and common sense instead of on formal policies, most of the time we would get better results, and at lower cost. If you're careful to hire people who will put the company's interests first, who understand and support the desire for a high-performance workplace, 97% of your employees will do the right thing. Most companies spend endless time and money writing and enforcing HR policies to deal with problems the other 3% might cause. Instead, we tried really hard to not hire those people, and we let them go if it turned out we'd made a hiring mistake.

Adultlike behavior means talking openly about issues with your boss, your colleagues, and your subordinates. It means recognizing that even in companies with reams of HR policies, those policies are frequently skirted as managers and their reports work out what makes sense on a case-by-case basis.

Let me offer two examples.

When Netflix launched, we had a standard paid-time-off policy: People got 10 vacation days, 10 holidays, and a few sick days. We used an honor system—employees kept track of the days they took off and let their managers know when they'd be out. After we went public, our auditors freaked. They said Sarbanes-Oxley mandated that we account for time off. We considered instituting a formal tracking system. But then Reed asked, "Are companies *required* to give time off? If not, can't we just handle it informally and skip the accounting rigmarole?" I did some research and found that, indeed, no California law governed vacation time.

So instead of shifting to a formal system, we went in the opposite direction: Salaried employees were told to take whatever time they felt was appropriate. Bosses and employees were asked to work it out with one another. (Hourly workers in call centers and warehouses were given a more structured policy.) We did provide some guidance. If you worked in accounting or finance, you shouldn't plan to be out during the beginning or the end of a quarter, because those were busy times. If you wanted 30 days off in a row, you needed to meet with HR. Senior leaders were urged to take vacations and to let people know about them—they were role models for the policy. (Most were happy to comply.) Some people worried about whether the system would be inconsistent—whether some bosses would allow tons of time off while others would be stingy. In general, I worried more about fairness than consistency, because the reality is that in any organization, the highest-performing and most valuable employees get more leeway.

We also departed from a formal travel and expense policy and decided to simply require adultlike behavior there, too. The company's expense policy is five words long: "Act in Netflix's best interests." In talking that through with employees, we said we expected them to spend company money frugally, as if it were their own. Eliminating a formal policy and forgoing expense account police shifted responsibility to frontline managers, where it belongs. It also reduced costs: Many large companies still use travel agents (and pay their fees) to book trips, as a way to enforce travel policies. They could save money by letting employees book their own trips online. Like most Netflix managers, I had to have conversations periodically with employees who ate at lavish restaurants (meals that would have been fine for sales or recruiting, but not for eating alone or with a Netflix colleague). We kept an eye on our IT guys, who were prone to buying a lot of gadgets. But overall we found that expense accounts are another area where if you create a clear expectation of responsible behavior, most employees will comply.

Tell the Truth About Performance

Many years ago we eliminated formal reviews. We had held them for a while but came to realize they didn't make sense—they were too ritualistic and too infrequent. So we asked managers and employees to have conversations about performance as an organic part of their work. In many functions—sales, engineering, product development—it's fairly obvious how well people are doing. (As companies develop better analytics to measure performance, this becomes even truer.) Building a bureaucracy and elaborate rituals around measuring performance usually doesn't improve it.

Traditional corporate performance reviews are driven largely by fear of litigation. The theory is that if you want to get rid of someone, you need a paper trail documenting a history of poor achievement. At many companies, low performers are placed on "Performance Improvement Plans." I detest PIPs. I think they're fundamentally dishonest: They never accomplish what their name implies.

One Netflix manager requested a PIP for a quality assurance engineer named Maria, who had been hired to help develop our streaming service. The technology was new, and it was evolving very quickly. Maria's job was to find bugs. She was fast, intuitive, and hardworking. But in time we figured out how to automate the QA tests. Maria didn't like automation and wasn't particularly good at it. Her new boss (brought in to create a world-class automation tools team) told me he wanted to start a PIP with her.

I replied, "Why bother? We know how this will play out. You'll write up objectives and deliverables for her to achieve, which she can't, because she lacks the skills. Every Wednesday you'll take time away from your real work to discuss (and document) her shortcomings. You won't sleep on Tuesday nights, because you'll know it will be an awful meeting, and the same will be true for her. After a few weeks there will be tears. This will go on for three months. The entire team will know. And at the end you'll fire her. None of this will make any sense to her, because for five years she's been consistently rewarded for being great at her job—a job that basically doesn't exist anymore. Tell me again how Netflix benefits?

"Instead, let's just tell the truth: Technology has changed, the company has changed, and Maria's skills no longer apply. This won't be a surprise to her: She's been in the trenches, watching the work around her shift. Give her a great severance package—which, when she signs the documents, will dramatically reduce (if not eliminate) the chance of a lawsuit." In my experience, people can handle anything as long as they're told the truth—and this proved to be the case with Maria.

When we stopped doing formal performance reviews, we instituted informal 360-degree reviews. We kept them fairly simple: People were asked to identify things that colleagues should stop, start, or continue. In the beginning we used an anonymous software system, but over time we shifted to signed feedback, and many teams held their 360s face-to-face.

HR people can't believe that a company the size of Netflix doesn't hold annual reviews. "Are you making this up just to upset us?" they ask. I'm not. If you talk simply and honestly about performance on a regular basis, you can get good results—probably better ones than a company that grades everyone on a five-point scale.

Crafting a Culture of Excellence

NETFLIX FOUNDER AND CEO Reed Hastings discusses the company's unconventional HR practices.

HBR: Why did you write the Netflix culture deck?

Hastings: It's our version of *Letters to a Young Poet* for budding entrepreneurs. It's what we wish we had understood when we started. More than 100 people at Netflix have made major contributions to the deck, and we have more improvements coming.

Many of the ideas in it seem like common sense, but they go against traditional HR practices. Why aren't companies more innovative when it comes to talent management?

As a society, we've had hundreds of years to work on managing industrial firms, so a lot of accepted HR practices are centered in that experience. We're just beginning to learn how to run creative firms, which is quite different. Industrial firms thrive on reducing variation (manufacturing errors); creative firms thrive on *increasing* variation (innovation).

What reactions have you gotten from your peers to steps such as abolishing formal vacation and performance review policies? In general, do you think other companies admire your HR innovations or look askance at them?

My peers are mostly in the creative sector, and many of the ideas in our culture deck came from them. We are all learning from one another.

Which idea in the culture deck was the hardest sell with employees?

"Adequate performance gets a generous severance package." It's a pretty blunt statement of our hunger for excellence.

Have any of your talent management innovations been total flops?

Not so far.

Patty talks about how leaders should model appropriate behaviors to help people adapt to an environment with fewer formal controls. With that in mind, how many days off did you take in 2013?

"Days off" is a very industrial concept, like being "at the office." I find Netflix fun to think about, so there are probably no 24-hour periods when I never think about work. But I did take three or four weeklong family trips over the past year, which were both stimulating and relaxing.

Managers Own the Job of Creating Great Teams

Discussing the military's performance during the Iraq War, Donald Rumsfeld, the former defense secretary, once famously said, "You go to war with the army you have, not the army you might want or wish to have at a later time." When I talk to managers about creating great teams, I tell them to approach the process in exactly the opposite way.

In my consulting work, I ask managers to imagine a documentary about what their team is accomplishing six months from now. What specific results do they see? How is the work different from what the team is doing today? Next I ask them to think about the skills needed to make the images in the movie become reality. Nowhere in the early stages of the process do I advise them to think about the team they actually have. Only after they've done the work of envisioning the ideal outcome and the skill set necessary to achieve it should they analyze how well their existing team matches what they need.

If you're in a fast-changing business environment, you're probably looking at a lot of mismatches. In that case, you need to have honest conversations about letting some team members find a place where their skills are a better fit. You also need to recruit people with the right skills.

We faced the latter challenge at Netflix in a fairly dramatic way as we began to shift from DVDs by mail to a streaming service. We had to store massive volumes of files in the cloud and figure out how huge numbers of people could reliably access them. (By some estimates, up to a third of peak residential internet traffic in the United States comes from customers streaming Netflix movies.) So we needed to find people deeply experienced with cloud services who worked for companies that operate on a giant scale—companies like Amazon, eBay, Google, and Facebook, which aren't the easiest places to hire someone away from.

Our compensation philosophy helped a lot. Most of its principles stem from ideals described earlier: Be honest, and treat people like adults. For instance, during my tenure Netflix didn't pay performance bonuses, because we believed that they're unnecessary if you hire the right people. If your employees are fully formed adults who put the company first, an annual bonus won't make them work harder or smarter. We also believed in market-based pay and would tell employees that it was smart to interview with competitors when they had the chance, in order to get a good sense of the market rate for their talent. Many HR people dislike it when employees talk to recruiters, but I always told employees to take the call, ask how much, and send me the number—it's valuable information.

In addition, we used equity compensation much differently from the way most companies do. Instead of larding stock options on top of a competitive salary, we let employees choose how much (if any) of their compensation would be in the form of equity. If employees wanted stock options, we reduced their salaries accordingly. We believed that they were sophisticated enough to understand the trade-offs, judge their personal tolerance for risk, and decide what was best for them and their families. We distributed options every month, at a slight discount from the market price. We had no vesting period—the options could be cashed in immediately. Most tech companies have a four-year vesting schedule and try to use options as "golden handcuffs" to aid retention, but we never thought that made sense. If you see a better opportunity elsewhere, you should be allowed to take what you've earned and leave. If you no longer want to work with us, we don't want to hold you hostage.

We continually told managers that building a great team was their most important task. We didn't measure them on whether they were excellent coaches or mentors or got their paperwork done on time. Great teams accomplish great work, and recruiting the right team was the top priority.

Leaders Own the Job of Creating the Company Culture

After I left Netflix and began consulting, I visited a hot startup in San Francisco. It had 60 employees in an open loft-style office with a foosball table, two pool tables, and a kitchen, where a chef cooked lunch for the entire staff. As the CEO showed me around, he talked about creating a fun atmosphere. At one point I asked him what the most important value for his company was. He replied, "Efficiency."

"OK," I said. "Imagine that I work here, and it's 2:58 p.m. I'm playing an intense game of pool, and I'm winning. I estimate that I can finish the game in five minutes. We have a meeting at 3:00. Should I stay and win the game or cut it short for the meeting?"

"You should finish the game," he insisted. I wasn't surprised; like many tech startups, this was a casual place, where employees wore hoodies and brought pets to work, and that kind of casualness often extends to punctuality. "Wait a second," I said. "You told me that efficiency is your most important cultural value. It's not efficient to delay a meeting and keep coworkers waiting because of a pool game. Isn't there a mismatch between the values you're talking up and the behaviors you're modeling and encouraging?"

When I advise leaders about molding a corporate culture, I tend to see three issues that need attention. This type of mismatch is one. It's a particular problem at startups, where there's a premium on casualness that can run counter to the high-performance ethos leaders want to create. I often sit in on company meetings to get a sense of how people operate. I frequently see CEOs who are clearly winging it. They lack a real agenda. They're working from slides that were obviously put together an hour before or were recycled from the previous round of VC meetings. Workers notice these things, and if they see a leader who's not fully prepared and who relies on charm, IQ, and improvisation, it affects how they perform, too. It's a waste of time to articulate ideas about values and culture if you don't model and reward behavior that aligns with those goals.

The second issue has to do with making sure employees understand the levers that drive the business. I recently visited a Texas startup whose employees were mostly engineers in their twenties. "I bet half the people in this room have never read a P&L," I said to the CFO. He replied, "It's true—they're not financially savvy or business savvy, and our biggest challenge is teaching them how the business works." Even if you've hired people who want to perform well, you need to clearly communicate how the company makes money and what behaviors will drive its success. At Netflix, for instance, employees used to focus too heavily on subscriber growth, without much awareness that our expenses often ran ahead of it: We were spending huge amounts buying DVDs, setting up distribution centers, and ordering original programming, all before we'd collected a cent from our new subscribers. Our employees needed to learn that even though revenue was growing, managing expenses really mattered.

The third issue is something I call the split personality startup. At tech companies this usually manifests itself as a schism between the engineers and the sales team, but it can take other forms. At Netflix, for instance, I sometimes had to remind people that there were big differences between the salaried professional staff at headquarters and the hourly workers in the call centers. At one point our finance team wanted to shift the whole company to direct-deposit paychecks, and I had to point out that some of our hourly workers didn't have bank accounts. That's a small example, but it speaks to a larger point: As leaders build a company culture, they need to be aware of subcultures that might require different management.

Good Talent Managers Think Like Businesspeople and Innovators First, and Like HR People Last

Throughout most of my career I've belonged to professional associations of human resources executives. Although I like the people in these groups personally, I often find myself disagreeing with them. Too many devote time to morale improvement initiatives. At some places entire teams focus on getting their firm onto lists of "Best Places to Work" (which, when you dig into the methodologies, are really based just on perks and benefits). At a recent conference I met someone from a company that had appointed a "chief happiness officer"—a concept that makes me slightly sick.

During 30 years in business I've never seen an HR initiative that improved morale. HR departments might throw parties and hand out T-shirts, but if the stock price is falling or the company's products aren't perceived as successful, the people at those parties will quietly complain—and they'll use the T-shirts to wash their cars.

Instead of cheerleading, people in my profession should think of themselves as businesspeople. What's good for the company? How do we communicate that to employees? How can we help every worker understand what we mean by high performance?

Here's a simple test: If your company has a performance bonus plan, go up to a random employee and ask, "Do you know specifically what you should be doing right now to increase your bonus?" If he or she can't answer, the HR team isn't making things as clear as they need to be.

At Netflix I worked with colleagues who were changing the way people consume filmed entertainment, which is an incredibly innovative pursuit—yet when I started there, the expectation was that I would default to mimicking other companies' best practices (many of them antiquated), which is how almost everyone seems to approach HR. I rejected those constraints. There's no reason the HR team can't be innovative too.

Originally published in January–February 2014. **Reprint** R1401E

Leading the Team You Inherit

by Michael D. Watkins

DAVID BENET HAD PROBLEMS TO SOLVE when he came in to lead the highest-growth unit at a large medical devices company. Although sales had increased when two new products launched the previous year, the numbers still fell short of expectations, given all the evidence of unmet customer needs. The company's future hinged on the success of both products—an instrument for inserting stents into blocked arteries and an electronic implant for stabilizing cardiac rhythm.

So the long-term stakes were high, and the team wasn't exactly humming. Stories about missed opportunities and hints of a toxic culture had drifted upward to senior management.

All those factors had prompted the decision to replace the unit's executive vice president with someone from the outside, and David fit the bill. He had a record of stellar accomplishments at a rival company, where he had turned around one business unit and accelerated the growth of another. But in taking on this new role, he faced a common challenge: He didn't get to handpick the people who would be working with him. Rather, he inherited his predecessor's team—the team that had created the situation David was hired to fix.

Indeed, most newly appointed leaders have limited familiarity with their teams at the outset and can't immediately swap in new people to help grow or transform the business. Sometimes they lack the necessary political power or resources to rapidly replace personnel, or the culture does not allow it. Often, existing team members are essential for running the business in the short term but not the right people to lead it into the future.

All this highlights the importance of figuring out how to work effectively with a team you have inherited. Fraught with trade-offs, the process is like repairing an airplane in midflight. You can't just shut down the plane's engines while you rebuild them—at least not without causing a crash. You need to maintain stability while moving ahead.

There are many frameworks to help leaders build new teams. One of the best known is "forming, storming, norming, and performing," created by Bruce Tuckman in 1965. According to Tuckman's model and more recent ones like it, teams go through predictable phases of development that, with the right interventions, can be accelerated. The problem is that these models assume leaders build their teams from scratch, carefully choosing members and setting direction from the very beginning.

In my work helping leaders navigate major transitions, I have found that most people, like David, instead need a framework for taking over and transforming a team. That's what this article provides. First, leaders must assess the human capital and group dynamics they have inherited, to get a clear picture of the current state. Next, they must reshape the team according to what's needed—looking with fresh eyes at its membership, sense of purpose and direction, operating model, and behavioral patterns. Finally, they can accelerate team development and improve performance by identifying opportunities for early wins and making plans to secure them.

Assessing the Team

When you are leading a new team, you must quickly determine whether you have the right people doing the right things in the right ways to propel the organization forward. From day one you will

Idea in Brief

What's Wrong

Most team-building frameworks assume that you get to cherry-pick members and set the direction and tone from day one. But leaders usually don't have that luxury; they must work with the people they inherit.

What's Needed

Leaders who are taking over and transforming a team need guidance on how to navigate the transition and improve performance.

What's Effective

Here's a three-step model that works: First, assess the people you've got and the dynamics at play. Second, reshape the team's membership, sense of purpose and direction, operating model, and behaviors according to the business challenges you face. Third, accelerate the team's development by scoring some early wins.

have a lot of demands on your time and attention, and those will only grow, so efficient team assessment is key.

It's important to be systematic, as well. Although most leaders inherit and size up many teams over their careers, few are deliberate about what they look for in people. Through experience they arrive at intuitive assessment criteria and methods—which are fine for familiar situations but otherwise problematic. Why? Because the characteristics of effective team members vary dramatically depending on the circumstances.

Your assessments will be faster and more accurate if you explicitly state your criteria. What qualities should people have in order to tackle the particular challenges your team faces? How important are diverse or complementary skills in the group? Which attributes do you think you can shape through your leadership? You may be able to improve people's engagement and focus, for example, but not their inherent trustworthiness. (See the sidebar "What Qualities Are You Looking For?")

Your requirements will depend partly on the state of the business. In a turnaround, you will seek people who are already up to speed—you won't have time to focus on skill building until things are more stable. If you are trying to sustain a team's success, however, it

What Qualities Are You Looking For?

LIKE MOST LEADERS, you may have a "gut" sense of what you typically look for in people. But different situations and challenges call for different strengths. This exercise will help you better understand and articulate your priorities each time you inherit a team.

Assign percentages to the qualities below, according to how much emphasis you think each should receive, given your current circumstances and goals. Make sure the numbers in the right column add up to 100.

Those numbers will be rough, of course. For some team members (say, your head of finance), competence may be the top priority; for others (say, your head of marketing), energy or people skills may be equally or more critical. The importance of the role and the state of the business may also affect your estimates.

When executives complete this exercise, they almost always give trustworthiness the most weight. That's because they view it as a sign of inherent character—not something that can be strengthened with good management. However, leaders do think they can help team members improve their focus and energy. So it's not surprising that they give those qualities less emphasis than trustworthiness early on.

What do your rankings say about what you value most right now and what you believe you can influence through leadership? Are any of the criteria go/no-go issues for you?

---

probably makes sense to develop high potentials, and you will have more time to do so.

Your expectations for team members will also be shaped by how essential their roles are to meeting your goals. People in critical positions will be assessed with greater urgency and higher standards. David Benet (names are disguised throughout) had two sales leaders, both deemed critical because their groups had to drive cardiologists' awareness of the new products. They both needed to be immediately effective at communicating the products' benefits to opinion leaders. The head of HR was a vital role, too—serious midlevel talent weaknesses in sales and marketing had to be addressed soon. The head of communications, however, wasn't as big a priority; reviews

Quality	Description	Importance
Competence	Has the technical expertise and experience to do the job effectively	
Trustworthiness	Can be relied upon to be straight with you and to follow through on commitments	
Energy	Brings the right attitude to the job (isn't burned-out or disengaged)	
People skills	Gets along well with others on the team and supports collaboration	
Focus	Sets priorities and sticks to them, instead of veering off in all directions	
Judgment	Exercises good sense, especially under pressure or when faced with making sacrifices for the greater good	
TOTAL		100%

of his work and conversations with colleagues revealed that he could be more innovative, but David decided to leave him in place for the time being.

Another factor to consider is to what degree your reports need to work as a team, and on what tasks. Ask yourself, "Will the people I supervise have to collaborate a lot, or is it OK if they operate mostly independently?" The answer will help determine how important it is for you to cultivate teamwork. Think of the people who typically report to a corporate treasurer, such as the heads of tax, cash management, and M&A analysis. These individuals should strive to operate as a high-performing group of managers who run their departments independently and effectively. Trying to turn that

Sizing Up People One-on-One

EARLY ONE-ON-ONE MEETINGS are a valuable tool for assessing the members of your new team. Depending on your style, these meetings might be informal discussions, formal reviews, or a combination, but you should approach them in a standard way.

Prepare

Review available personnel history, performance data, and appraisals. Familiarize yourself with each person's skills so that you can assess how he functions on the team and with his own unit or group. Observe how team members interact. Do relations appear cordial and productive? Tense and competitive? Explain to everyone that you will be using the meetings to assess the whole team and individual members.

Create an Interview Template

Ask people the same questions, and see how their insights vary. For example, What are the strengths and weaknesses of our existing strategy? What are our biggest challenges and opportunities in the short term? In the medium term? What resources could we leverage more effectively? How could we improve the way the team works together? If you were in my position, what would your priorities be?

group into a team through classic activities like creating a shared vision and establishing common performance goals and metrics would just frustrate everyone, because little or no collaborative work needs to be done. In such situations, assessment and management would focus more on individual performance and less on ability to work together. David, however, had a team of functional leaders who were quite interdependent. For example, he needed his VPs of sales, marketing, and communications to work closely together on refining and executing go-to-market strategies for the two products. So he had to gauge their relationships and collaborative capabilities.

To conduct an effective assessment, you'll hold a mix of one-on-one and team meetings, supplementing with input from key stakeholders such as customers, suppliers, and colleagues outside the team. (See the sidebar "Sizing Up People One-on-One.") You'll

Look for Verbal and Nonverbal Clues

Notice what people say and don't say. Do they volunteer information, or do you have to extract it? Do they take responsibility for problems, make excuses, or point fingers at others? You should also look for inconsistencies between people's words and their body language. That sort of mismatch can signal dishonesty or distrust of management—and either way, it needs to be addressed. Pay attention as well to topics that elicit strong emotions. Those hot buttons provide clues about what motivates people and what kinds of changes would energize them.

Summarize and Share What You Learn

After you've interviewed everyone, discuss your findings with the team. This will demonstrate that you are coming up to speed quickly. If your feedback highlights differences of opinion or raises uncomfortable issues, you'll also have a chance to observe the team under a modest amount of stress. Watching how people respond may lead to valuable insight into team culture and power dynamics.

also look at team members' individual track records and performance evaluations. Those didn't turn up any immediate red flags for David—but he knew the team had underperformed. His meetings helped him determine why and what to do about it.

It soon became clear that he had two significant personnel issues. The first was Carlos, the VP of surgical sales. Carlos had the longest tenure with the company and a seemingly tight connection with the CEO. However, his performance on the new surgical product had been lackluster. More important, comments from his peers and direct reports pointed to a micromanaging leadership style that undermined morale in his group and revealed a lack of collaboration with the rest of the team. For instance, he was hoarding information that could have been valuable to the interventional sales group and to the marketing people, and this was poisoning team dynamics.

Henry, the VP of human resources, presented a different challenge. He would have been a solid HR leader in normal circumstances, because he was skilled at handling typical challenges associated with hiring, performance management, and compensation and benefits. But he was not well suited to the demands of a high-growth environment. David reviewed the work Henry had done on talent appraisal and succession planning and rated it a B at best.

After completing his assessment, David decided that he would retain most of his team members, whose tenure with the company varied from five years to more than 25. But he knew he had to work on people's attitudes—especially the lack of trust between functions.

Reshaping the Team

Post-assessment, the next task is to reshape the team within the constraints of the organization's culture, the leader's mandate, and the available talent. Ultimately new leaders want their people to exhibit high-performance behaviors such as sharing information freely, identifying and dealing with conflict swiftly, solving problems creatively, supporting one another, and presenting a unified face to the outside world once decisions have been made. Leaders can promote these behaviors by focusing on four factors: the team's composition, its alignment with a shared vision, its operating model, and its integration of new rules and expectations.

Composition

The most obvious way to reshape a team is to replace underperformers and anyone whose capabilities are not a good match for the situation. But this can be difficult culturally and politically, and in many cases, it's simply not possible—leaders must work with the people they inherit. Even when employees can be let go and newcomers brought in, the process takes time and consumes energy. So doing this in the first few months should be reserved for dire business situations, for employees in critical roles who clearly cannot do the work, or for truly toxic personalities that are undermining the enterprise.

Fortunately, you can reshape team composition in other ways. For instance, you might wait for normal turnover to create space for the types of people you want. This usually takes time, but you may be able to speed up the process by signaling your expectations of higher performance—thus encouraging marginal performers to seek other roles. You can also watch for positions in other areas of the organization that might suit people who are valuable but not a good match for your team.

Another option is to groom high potentials to take on new responsibilities, provided you have enough time and other resources. If not, you may instead choose to alter individuals' roles to better match their capabilities. This powerful, often underappreciated way of reshaping teams may involve adjusting the scope of existing roles, having people swap jobs, or creating new positions by carving up the work differently. Any of these tactics can revitalize people who have become stale in their jobs, but few leaders think of trying alternative ways of allocating work.

David used a mix of these approaches to change the composition of his team. He concluded that Carlos, the VP of surgical sales, was undermining effectiveness and needed to leave. After consulting with senior management and corporate HR, David offered him a generous early retirement package, eliminated his role, and restructured the sales groups under a single VP. He appointed Carlos's counterpart in interventional sales, Lois, to lead the unified sales organization. To help Lois succeed in the bigger role, David asked HR to enroll her in an intensive leadership development program that included coaching.

David's other major move on personnel was to find a new position in the company for Henry, his VP of human resources. Fortunately, the corporate compensation and benefits group had an opening that was a great fit, and Henry gladly took it, feeling somewhat burned out from the stresses David's unit had experienced. That allowed David to search for a new VP with the talent planning, acquisition, and development capabilities needed to strengthen the lower levels of the sales and marketing organizations.

Alignment

You will also need to ensure that everyone has a clear sense of purpose and direction. Sometimes a team's stated direction needs to be changed. In other cases, it's more or less right, but people are just not pulling together.

To get everyone aligned, the team must agree on answers to four basic questions:

What will we accomplish? You spell this out in your mission, goals, and key metrics.

Why should we do it? Here is where your vision statement and incentives come into play.

How will we do it? This includes defining the team's strategy in relation to the organization's, as well as sorting out the plans and activities needed for execution.

Who will do what? People's roles and responsibilities must support all of the above.

Generally leaders are more comfortable with alignment than with other aspects of reshaping, because they have well-established tools and processes for tackling it. But one element in particular tends to trip them up: the "why." If the team lacks a clear and compelling vision that inspires them, and if members lack the proper incentives, they probably won't move energetically in the right direction. Compensation and benefits aren't sufficient motivators on their own. You need to offer a full set of rewards, including interesting work, status, and potential for advancement.

This can be challenging, for a couple of reasons: It's often hard to discern when *hidden* incentives (like competing commitments to other teams) are getting in the way. And you may have limited influence on certain rewards, as is often the case with compensation.

During individual assessment interviews and in group discussions, David had discovered that people weren't as aligned on goals, metrics, and incentives as they needed to be. Specifically, the two sales forces had no incentives to help each other. In addition, the marketing teams for the two products were underresourced and competing for available funding in dysfunctional ways.

To get his team members striving for the same things, David worked with them to develop a comprehensive dashboard of metrics that could be reviewed on a regular basis. He also realigned the team with the rest of the company by raising the performance bar to match the executive committee's expectations. In the business planning process, he committed the team to achieving a higher level of growth. Perhaps most important, he addressed the issue of misaligned incentives that had created conflict between the two sales groups. With that function now unified, he and Lois restructured the sales force on a geographic basis so that individual salespeople represented both of the new products and were rewarded accordingly.

Operating model

Reshaping a team also involves rethinking how and when people come together to do the work. This may include increasing or decreasing the number of "core" members, creating subteams, adjusting the types and frequency of meetings, running meetings differently, and designing new protocols for follow-up.

Such changes can be powerful levers for improving team performance. Unfortunately, many new leaders either continue to operate the way their predecessors did or make only small adjustments. To think more creatively about your team's operating model, identify your real constraints on how the work gets done—such as established business planning and budgeting processes for the entire enterprise—and then ask yourself how the team could operate within them more efficiently and productively. In addition, consider whether it makes sense to create subteams (formal or informal) to improve collaboration among interdependent members. Also think about whether certain activities require more-frequent attention than others. This will help you establish a meeting cadence that works, both for the team as a whole and for any subteams.

David recognized key interdependencies among sales, marketing, and communications, so he set up a subteam of leaders from those functions. To get more-focused attention and faster feedback from them, he decided to meet with them weekly, while holding full-team meetings only every other month and reserving those for information sharing and discussion of strategic issues. The subteam oversaw efforts to refine and execute go-to-market strategies for the two products—David's immediate priority. The work was done by cross-functional teams consisting of the sales, marketing, and communications leaders' direct reports. Streamlining processes, increasing collaboration, and speeding up reaction times—combined with the restructuring of the sales force and additional funding for the marketing teams—rapidly increased sales growth.

When rethinking meeting frequency and agendas, it helps to understand the three types of meetings that leadership teams typically have—strategic, operational, and learning—so that you can allocate an appropriate amount of time to each. *Strategic* meetings concern the biggest decisions that need to be made—about business models, vision, strategy, organizational configurations, and so on. Though they tend to be relatively infrequent, they require time for in-depth discussion. *Operational* meetings involve reviewing forecasts and measures of short-term performance, and adjusting activities and plans in light of those results. These are usually shorter and more frequent than strategic meetings. *Learning* meetings are scheduled on an as-needed basis, often after crises or in response to emerging issues. They can also focus on team building.

When teams try to jam all these activities into a single recurring meeting, operational urgencies tend to crowd out strategic and learning discussions. By thinking through the right mix of meeting types and scheduling each kind on its own regular cycle, you can prevent that problem. It's typically best to work out a rhythm for your operational meetings first, deciding how frequent they should be and who should participate. Then you can overlay the less-frequent strategic meetings, allowing plenty of time for discussion. Finally, you should establish what kinds of events will trigger the ad hoc learning meetings. You might, for example, decide to hold them after any major market event, such as the introduction of a competing product, or in the wake of a significant internal failure, such as a product recall.

Integration

The final element of reshaping is integration. This involves establishing ground rules and processes to feed and sustain desired behaviors and serving as a role model for your team members. Of course, the team's composition, alignment, and operating model also influence members' behavior. But focusing on those elements isn't sufficient, especially when leaders inherit teams with negative group dynamics. Those situations require remedial work: changing the destructive patterns of behavior and fostering a sense of shared purpose.

That was the case with David's team. The infighting between the marketing and sales VPs, combined with the previous leader's inability to curb Carlos's bad behavior or secure resources, had eroded members' trust. Once David restructured sales, the team realized that he was a decisive straight shooter (unlike his predecessor). He also earned respect with the changes he made in team membership and the funding he obtained for marketing. So he was in a good position to rebuild trust. He began by commissioning a more focused assessment of team dynamics; the time was right for a deeper dive on this, now that he had been in his role a bit longer and had established credibility with the group. This independent, expert evaluation included an anonymous survey of team members and follow-up interviews that zeroed in on the key elements of trust within leadership teams:

- confidence that all team members have the capabilities to do their jobs

- transparency in sharing information

- belief that commitments will be honored

- psychological safety to express divergent opinions without fear of belittlement, criticism, or retribution

- security that confidences will be maintained

- unity around decisions once people agree to them

The evaluation revealed that transparency, psychological safety, and unity were the primary trust issues for the team. To communicate those results, David brought everyone together for an offsite. He pointed out that they would never be a winning team if the trust problems persisted. He also shared what he had found to be the structural causes (misaligned incentives, underfunding, Carlos's impact) and what had already been done to address them. Crucially, he expressed confidence that the unit could become a high-performing team—and he voiced his commitment to making that happen.

David then laid out a process for reshaping group dynamics. First, everybody would agree on certain behavioral principles: They would share information, treat one another with respect, and act as "one team" after decisions were made. Then they would approach decision making with greater transparency. For each decision, he would communicate up front whether he would make the call, open it up to a small group, or seek full-team consensus.

After the offsite, David focused on "living" these new principles and processes himself. He also reinforced desired behaviors. And when he saw any unproductive behaviors emerge, he intervened immediately—either in team meetings or privately with individuals. Although it took time, because old habits die hard, the group dynamics improved.

David was careful to revisit these principles and processes when his new VP of HR joined the team. Revisiting and reinforcing behavioral expectations should be standard practice any time there is a change in team membership or mission. It's also valuable to schedule a regular (quarterly or semiannual) review of how the team is functioning and whether the principles are being upheld.

Accelerating the Team's Development

Building on their assessment and reshaping work, leaders need to energize team members with some early wins. As David knew from experience, this increases people's confidence in their capabilities and reinforces the value of their new rules and processes. He and his team started by setting challenging goals for the next three months' sales; then they set about delivering. They specified the work involved and who was accountable for it, determined which external stakeholders' support was essential, allocated responsibility for building relationships, and developed messages and methods for sharing results with the rest of the organization. They exceeded their goals by a substantial margin.

Once the team had those successes in place, it kept building on them. The result was a virtuous cycle of achievement and confidence. By the end of David's first year, sales growth had far outstripped targets. In fact, already-ambitious forecasts had to be revised upward three times. The executive committee was understandably delighted by the progress, which created an opening for David to secure additional resources, expand the sales force, and exceed the usual salary limits to hire outstanding talent. The growth trajectory continued for the next two years, until competitors' introductions of new products began to make things more challenging. By that time, however, David's team had achieved a dominant position in the market, and it was ready to launch new products of its own.

Originally published in June 2016. Reprint R1606D

The Overcommitted Organization

by Mark Mortensen and Heidi K. Gardner

A SENIOR EXECUTIVE WE'LL CALL Christine is overseeing the launch of Analytix, her company's new cloud-based big-data platform, and she's expected to meet a tight go-live deadline. Until two weeks ago, her team was on track to do that, but it has since fallen seriously behind schedule. Her biggest frustration: Even though nothing has gone wrong with Analytix, her people keep getting pulled into other projects. She hasn't seen her three key engineers for days, because they've been busy fighting fires around a security breach on another team's product. Now she has to explain to the CEO that she can't deliver as promised—at a time when the company badly needs a successful launch.

Christine's story is hardly unique. Across the world, senior managers and team leaders are increasingly frustrated by conflicts arising from what we refer to as multiteaming—having their people assigned to multiple projects simultaneously. But given the significant benefits of multiteaming, it has become a way of organizational life, particularly in knowledge work. It allows groups to share individuals' time and brainpower across functional and departmental lines. It increases efficiency, too. Few organizations can afford to have their employees focus on just one project at a time and sit idle between tasks. So companies have optimized human capital somewhat as they would machines in factories, spreading expensive resources across teams that don't need 100% of those resources

100% of the time. As a result, they avoid costly downtime during projects' slow periods, and they can bring highly specialized experts in-house to dip in and out of critical projects as needed. Multiteaming also provides important pathways for knowledge transfer and the dissemination of best practices throughout organizations.

As clear and quantifiable as these advantages are, the costs are substantial and need to be managed, as Christine would attest. Organizations open themselves up to the risk of transmitting shocks across teams when shared members link the fates of otherwise independent projects. And teams discover that the constant entrance and exit of members weakens group cohesion and identity, making it harder to build trust and resolve issues. Individual employees pay a big price as well. They often experience stress, fatigue, and burnout as they struggle to manage their time and engagement across projects.

Over the past 15 years, we have studied collaboration in hundreds of teams, in settings as varied as professional services, oil and gas, high tech, and consumer goods. (See the sidebar "About the Research.") By carefully observing people during various stages of project-driven work, we have learned a tremendous amount about multiteaming. In this article we discuss why it is so prevalent in today's economy, examine the key problems that crop up for organizational and team leaders, and provide recommendations for how to solve them.

Why This Matters Now

Even though assigning employees to multiple projects at once is not new, the practice is especially widespread today. In a survey of more than 500 managers in global companies, we found that 81% of those working on teams worked on more than one concurrently. Other research places the number even higher—for example, 95% in knowledge-intensive industries.

Why is multiteaming practically ubiquitous? For several reasons.

First, organizations must draw on expertise in multiple disciplines to solve many large, complex problems. Businesses are tackling

Idea in Brief

The Pros

By assigning people to multiple teams at once, organizations make efficient use of time and brain-power. They also do a better job of solving complex problems and sharing knowledge across groups.

The Cons

Competing priorities and other conflicts can make it hard for teams with overlapping membership to stay on track. Group cohesion often suffers. And

people who belong to many teams at once may experience burnout, which hurts engagement and performance.

The Fixes

Leaders can mitigate these risks by building trust and familiarity through launches and skills mapping, identifying which groups are most vulnerable to shocks, improving coordination across teams, and carving out more opportunities for learning.

cybersecurity risks that span departments as diverse as finance, supply chain, and travel. Energy companies are coordinating global megaprojects, including the opening of new deep-sea resource fields. Transportation and logistics firms are tasked with getting resources from point A to point B on time, irrespective of how remote those points are or what is being delivered. Large-scale manufacturing and construction endeavors, such as aircraft and city infrastructure projects, require tight collaboration between those producing the work and the agencies regulating it. In such contexts, organizations can't rely on generalists to come up with comprehensive, end-to-end solutions. They must combine the contributions of experts with deep knowledge in various domains. (For more on this, see "Getting Your Stars to Collaborate," HBR, January–February 2017.)

Second, with crowded markets and reduced geographic and industry barriers, organizations now face greater pressure to keep costs down and stretch resources. One client manager in a professional services firm noted, "To be really good stewards of client dollars, we don't want to pay for five weeks of a specialist's time when what we really need is an intense effort from that person in week five." That's why "bench time" between projects and even slow periods during projects have become increasingly rare. The instant

About the Research

OVER THE PAST 15 YEARS, we've been measuring both the benefits and the trade-offs of multiteaming in areas such as human capital, resource utilization, quality management, and customer satisfaction. We have conducted:

- **In-depth studies** of eight global professional services firms where multiteaming is the norm, including statistical analyses of their staffing databases and personnel records.

- **A survey** of more than 500 midlevel managers in global companies, representing a wide range of industries and professions, to examine trends across organizations and geographies.

- **Ongoing research** at a 5,000-person technology and services company that is trying to optimize multiteaming. So far, this includes more than 50 interviews with team leaders and executives. We're also designing organizational experiments to test best practices and collect data on outcomes such as efficiency, staff burnout, and customer satisfaction.

- **Ongoing research** on agent-based modeling to understand the behavior of large systems of interconnected teams. We are also using simulations to model multiteaming, with a focus on understanding the relationship between team size, percentage of overlap among teams, and the number of teams each team member is on.

people are underutilized, their organizations put them to work on other things. In our research we found that even senior-level managers were flipping among seven or more projects in a single day—and as many as 25 in a given week. Compounding this, technology makes it easier to track downtime—even if it's just minutes—and assign employees work or loop them into projects during any lulls.

Third, organizational models are moving away from hierarchical, centralized staffing to give employees more choice in their projects and improve talent development, engagement, and retention. Indeed, in the gig economy, individuals have greater control than ever over the work they do (think open-source software programmers). This has made leading teams an even more critical skill. (For more on this, see "The Secrets of Great Teamwork," HBR, June 2016.) At the same time, it has brought multiteaming—and the associated risks—to a whole new level. More and more people have at-will contracts and work not only on multiple projects but for multiple organizations. In many cases, companies are sharing team members' time and smarts with market rivals.

Although most managers recognize the increasing prevalence of multiteaming, few have a complete understanding of how it affects their organizations, their teams, and individual employees. For instance, top leaders in one professional services firm were surprised to learn who in their organization was most squeezed by multiteaming. First-year associates worked on as many as six projects in a week, which at a glance seemed like a lot. But the number rose steeply with tenure—employees worked on as many as 15 projects a week once they had reached the six-year mark. More-experienced people were members of fewer concurrent teams, but the more senior they got, the more likely they were to lead many projects at the same time. (See the exhibit "Who's feeling the pain?") Interviews revealed that working on multiple teams was stressful—one person likened it to being "slapped about" by different project leaders—despite benefits such as bringing lessons from one project to bear on others.

It's a classic "blind men and elephant problem." Managers see some of the benefits and some of the drawbacks firsthand but rarely all at once, because those things play out through different mechanisms and at different levels. Imagine, for example, a sales manager who wants to provide better solutions for customers by incorporating insights from her team members' experiences on other projects. That's not going to happen if splitting each individual's time across five projects means her team doesn't have the bandwidth to sit down and share those great ideas in the first place. Or consider a project manager who is thinking about adding a third engineer to his team—just 10% of a full-time equivalent—to reduce the load on his two overworked lead engineers. He may not recognize that this sort of slicing and dicing is the reason his first two engineers are in danger of burnout—they are being pulled into too many competing projects. Examples like these abound.

For the most part, the benefits of multiteaming involve efficiency and knowledge flow, while the costs are largely intra- or interpersonal and psychological. That may be why the costs are tracked and

Who's feeling the pain?

At one professional services firm, the employees most squeezed by multiteaming were midtenure associates—they helped with more and more projects as they gained experience. But the more senior people became, the more likely they were to lead many projects at the same time.

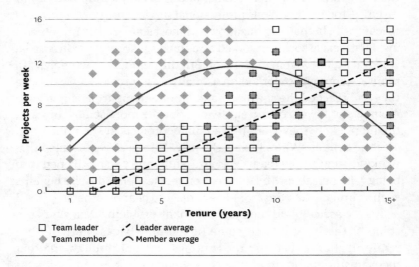

managed less closely, if at all—and why they so often undermine the benefits without leaders' realizing it.

Managing the Challenges

Through our research and consulting, we have identified several ways that both team and organizational leaders can reduce the costs of multiteaming and better capitalize on its benefits. We'll outline them below.

Priorities for team leaders

Coordinating members' efforts (both within and across teams) and promoting engagement and adaptability are the key challenges for

Goals of multiteaming
(And the challenges that can undermine them)

Goals for teams	Challenges
Cost savings, because team members whose expertise is not required at the moment can bill their downtime to other projects **Process improvements** as a result of importing best practices and insights through shared members	Weakened relationships and coherence within teams and projects Stress and burnout, particularly when members end up with assignments that exceed 100% time commitment Interteam coordination costs so that schedules of projects with shared members don't collide Rocky transitions as members switch between *tasks* where their contributions are defined relative to other members' skills, adjust to different *roles* (boss on one team but subordinate on another), and learn new team *contexts* with unfamiliar routines, symbols, jokes, expectations, tolerance for ambiguity, and so on Reduced learning, because members lack time together to share knowledge and ideas Reduced motivation, because members have a small percentage of their time dedicated to any given project
Goals for organizations	**Challenges**
The capability to solve complex problems with members who have deep, specialized knowledge **Improved resource utilization** across projects (no one is dedicated to a project that needs only 5% of his or her time) **Increased knowledge transfer** and learning through shared membership	Politics and tensions over shared human resources Coordination costs of aligning timelines of projects even when they are not linked by content or workflow Weakened identification with the organization if people feel commoditized Increased risk as shocks affecting one team may pull shared members off other projects

team leaders. Focusing on those goals early on, before your team even meets for the first time, will help you establish stronger relationships, reduce coordination costs, ease the friction of transitions, ward off political skirmishes, and identify risks so that you can better mitigate them. Here's how to do it:

Launch the team well to establish trust and familiarity. When fully dedicated to one team, people learn about their teammates' outside lives—family, hobbies, life events, and the like. This enables them to coordinate better (they know, for example, that one teammate is off-line during kids' bedtimes or that another routinely hits the gym during lunch). More important, it forges strong bonds and interpersonal trust, which team members need in order to seek and offer constructive feedback, introduce one another to valuable network connections, and rely on one another's technical expertise.

When multiteaming, in contrast, people tend to be hyperfocused on efficiency and are less inclined to share personal information. If you don't engineer personal interactions *for* them, chances are they'll be left with an anemic picture of their teammates, which can breed suspicion about why others fail to respond promptly, how committed they are to team outcomes, and so on. So make sure team members spend some time in the beginning getting to know their colleagues. This will also help far-flung contributors give one another the benefit of the doubt later on. A Boston-based designer told us about his British counterpart:

> I used to think that Sylvia was frosty and elitist, because she never jumped into our brainstorming sessions. Instead, she sent missives afterward, sometimes only to the project director. Then we spent a few days working together in person while I was in London, and I came to appreciate that she's an introvert who just needs time to process ideas before responding. Plus, because she had never met any of us, it was really hard for her to keep track of who had said what on the calls; she recognized only the leader's unique accent.

After the designer shared that "aha" with the team leader, the group switched to video calls so that everyone could see Sylvia's "thinking face" and she could feel confident that she was responding to the right people when making comments.

Formally launching the team—in person, if at all possible—helps a lot, especially if members open up about their own development goals. At McKinsey each team member, including the leader, explains how he or she expects to use that project to build or improve a critical skill. This level of openness not only encourages people to display some vulnerability (which is practically the definition of trust) but also gives members concrete ideas about how they can help one another.

The launch may feel like an unnecessary step if people know one another and everyone is ready to dive in, but research shows that team kickoffs can improve performance by up to 30%, in part because they increase peer-to-peer accountability. By clarifying roles and objectives up front and establishing group norms, you're letting people know what to expect from their colleagues. That's needed on any team, of course, but it's especially critical in organizations where people belong to several teams at once and must absorb *many* sets of roles, objectives, and norms to do good work across the board.

On teams that people frequently join or leave, you'll need to periodically "re-kick" to onboard new members and assess whether agreed-upon processes and expectations still make sense. A good rule of thumb is to do this whenever 15% of the team has changed.

Map everyone's skills. Figure out the full portfolio of capabilities that each person brings to the project—both technical skills and broader kinds of knowledge, such as familiarity with the customer's decision-making process, or a knack for negotiation, or insights about an important target market. Make sure everyone knows how each teammate contributes. This increases the chances that members will learn from one another. The pride people take in sharing their knowledge and the cohesion fostered by peer mentoring are often as valuable as the actual knowledge shared.

As with launching, it's tempting to skip mapping if many members have worked together before. But we've found that even familiar teams are likely to hold outdated assumptions about individuals' potential contributions and often disagree about their teammates' expertise. As a result, they may argue about which roles members should play or bristle at assignments, thinking they're unfair or a bad fit. People may also waste time seeking outside resources when a teammate already has the needed knowledge, which demotivates those whose skills have been overlooked.

Sherif, a tax expert, experienced these problems when he joined with four colleagues to pitch a new client. "We'd all worked together on prior projects over the years—enough, we assumed, to know one another's 'sweet spots,'" he told us. "Over time, though, I grew more and more frustrated that two of my partners kept adding bits of regulatory advice to the pitch document—that's why I was on the team! I was handling nearly the exact same issue for a current client. I felt undermined, and the more they tried to sideline me, the more cantankerous I got." A few days before the client meeting, the group talked it out and discovered that Sherif had been honing his specialist expertise on projects the others hadn't been part of. They simply didn't realize what he had to offer. "We'd all been running in so many directions at the same time that our individual knowledge was changing quickly," he says. "No wonder we had friction."

Skills mapping could have prevented this. It also streamlines communication (no need to "reply all" if you know who's actually responsible for an issue). And it equips members to hold one another accountable for high-quality, on-time delivery, which is otherwise tricky when people are frequently coming and going. Creating the expectation of peer accountability relieves you as the team leader from some of that day-to-day oversight, freeing you up to scan the environment for potential shocks from other teams, for example, or to handle some of the inevitable negotiations about shared resources.

Manage time across teams. As you form a team, explicitly talk about everyone's competing priorities up front. By preemptively identifying crunch periods across projects, you can revamp deadlines or plan on spending more hands-on time yourself at certain points. Making the topic "discussable" so that people won't feel guilty about conflicts allows the team to openly and productively handle these issues when they come up later.

Establishing the right rhythm of meetings will make it easier to manage time across teams and address competing priorities. At the outset, you'll want to schedule several full-team meetings at critical junctures. (Research shows, for instance, that the halfway point in any project is a vital moment for a check-in, because that's when people shift into a higher gear, acutely aware that their time is limited.) Make attendance truly mandatory, and ensure it by giving each team member a piece of the meetings to run—even if it's just for 10 minutes. Check in early to see that all members have cleared meeting dates with their other teams. Ideally, the organizational culture will support formal check-in meetings as a high priority. If not, you may need to coordinate with other team leaders before putting a schedule together.

When you plan other team meetings, invite exactly who's needed and no one else, to minimize scheduling conflicts with other teams. Most of the time, you won't need everyone. Meet in subteams whenever possible. Don't forget to leverage technology: Instead of using precious live meeting time for updates, send a three-line e-mail or keep an online dashboard updated so that people can track progress as needed. Although technology doesn't replace face-to-face interaction, it can tide you over when a full meeting is too costly. And be creative: Younger team members are more likely to watch a 30-second video update than to read a two-page memo. Brief, spontaneous check-ins with team members over Skype or FaceTime can keep you updated on their competing deadlines; this visual interaction makes it more likely that you'll pick up cues about their stress and motivation levels, too.

Create a learning environment. Learning makes work feel more meaningful, and it's supposed to be a major benefit of multiteaming—but it often gets crowded out by time pressures.

There are other obstacles as well: Even if you've worked to build trust and personal connections, it's harder for multiteamers to give effective feedback than it is for dedicated team members, because people whose time is divided among several projects are less likely to regularly observe their teammates' actions or to be present at a time that "feels right" to offer critiques. Members who see only a small slice of a project may lack the context to fully understand what kind of feedback is appropriate. They also tend to focus on short-term tasks and to communicate with one another only when required.

Carrie, for example, was promoted to run the development office of a major metropolitan hospital, and her new 20-person staff was splitting its time among dozens of projects each week. After six months she realized, "We were all living in a feedback desert. I literally hadn't had a single comment in half a year about how I could do my job better, despite clear examples of projects that hadn't lived up to expectations." To change the tone, she modeled seeking input and responding to it constructively. "Doing so day in and day out, I started to create an environment where people shared their concerns to get help as soon as they needed it," she says. "Over time, it felt safe enough to put in more-formal processes to review projects and allow everyone to learn from errors without fear of retribution or blame."

You can also designate team members from different functions or offices to colead parts of the project so that they benefit from greater cross-contact; a formal assignment makes it more likely that they'll devote time to learning from each other. Similarly, pair a highly experienced team member with someone more junior and help them understand what both can gain from the exchange—it's not just one-way learning flowing down to the junior person.

Foster curiosity by posing "What if . . . ?" questions when it's likely that different members' backgrounds will provide new insights. If you get a question that you know another member could answer more fully, given his or her experience, redirect the asker and prompt the expert to do a bit of tutoring.

Boost motivation. On traditional, fixed teams, a strong sense of cohesion and group identity motivates members. But leaders in multiteaming environments need to leverage more of an exchange relationship. The ability to get jazzed about a project naturally flags when members spend only a small amount of time on it. Their inner accountant asks, "If I'll get only 10% of the credit, how much time and effort should I devote to this?" Figure out what your ten-percenters really value and frame the work in terms of those rewards. For example, if you have a Millennial who is eager to develop transferable skills, you might occasionally take time during meetings to have team members share and learn something new, or hold a workshop at the end of the project in which members cross-train.

Remember, too, that a sense of fairness drives many behaviors. If people feel they are pulling their weight while others slack off, they quickly become demotivated. When team members are tugged in many directions, it's often difficult for each one to recognize and appreciate how hard the others are working. As the leader, keep publicly acknowledging various members' contributions so that they become visible to the whole team, spawning a greater awareness of the collective efforts.

Like Christine, the frustrated leader of the Analytix software team, you might be feeling the strain of sharing valuable talent with other teams. Before you reach the breaking point, take these steps to clarify and manage your interdependency with other teams. They will help you avoid conflicts when that's possible, defuse them when it's not, and set an example of better collaboration with other team leaders—peers who face the same challenges you do.

Priorities for organizational leaders

If you're leading an organization where multiteaming is prevalent, you'll need to keep a close eye on how—and how many—members are shared across teams. We've found that you can reduce organizational risk and boost innovation by following these steps:

Map and analyze human capital interdependence. Patterns of team overlap range from highly concentrated (a large proportion of members are shared by just a few teams) to highly dispersed (the sharing is spread out across many teams).

Each pattern has its own implications for risk management. When a surprise problem jolts one team, the cry "All hands on deck" pulls shared members off their other teams—with disproportionately large effects on teams that have a concentrated overlap in members. When the overlap is more dispersed, the shock will be felt by more teams but to a lesser extent by each one. (See the exhibit "Who takes the hit?")

There are implications for knowledge transfer as well. Best practices travel from one project to the next as team members share what's working—and what isn't—on their other projects. Highly concentrated overlap makes it easier to spread ideas from one team to another; highly dispersed overlap makes it easier to spread them to more teams.

Who takes the hit?

When a couple of teams share many members, a shock to one group severely jolts the other, because people shift their efforts from ongoing work to firefighting.

When many teams share just one or two members, a shock to one group has a minor impact on the others—but the effects ripple throughout the organization.

Keep an accurate map of the links among teams in your organization through periodic updates from managers and team members. The frequency of these check-ins will depend on the life cycles of your teams. You'll need them more often if teams and assignments change week to week, less often if you've got yearlong projects with stable membership. This bird's-eye view will help you see which teams fail to pick up on new trends because they're too isolated, for instance, and which are so tightly interconnected that they aren't mitigating the risks of their shared membership.

The question we get most often about mapping interdependence is "What's the right amount?" Unfortunately, there's no magic answer—either for overlap between teams or for the number of teams per individual. Both targets depend highly on context. When teams are very similar in their tasks and culture, transitioning between them is relatively easy, so you can have a large amount of overlap and members can be on more of them. Transitioning across teams with very different tasks or cultures should be kept to a minimum, however—it's a bigger, costlier shift. Interestingly, the reverse holds true when workloads differ across teams, because members aren't in high demand from all teams at the same time (they aren't as susceptible to burnout as, say, tax advisers in April are).

Once you've done all this analysis, it's time to address the shortcomings you've uncovered—which brings us to the next two steps.

Promote knowledge flows. Pay close attention to teams that share few or no members with others—whether that's by design or by accident. These "islands" will require help staying informed about what's working elsewhere in the organization, sharing their knowledge and ideas, and deciding who would be the best resource to apply to a given task.

Your goal here is to establish knowledge transfer as a cultural norm, which involves getting employees to recognize that everyone wins when they take the time to share insights across projects. As with any cultural shift, it's important to lead by example and to reward those who follow suit. That's simple to say—but not so simple to do. To make it easier, highlight the benefits of sharing, and provide processes and technology to facilitate it, such as brown-bag lunches and online forums. One tech firm we worked with made a point of celebrating project breakthroughs that were attributed to transferred best practices. R&D teams at a manufacturing company shared monthly testimonials from individuals who had gained new insights through cross-staffing. In both cases the objective was to make the benefits of knowledge transfer clear—and to counter the ever-present pressure for people to keep their heads down and focus on immediate tasks.

Buffer against shocks. How can you prevent shocks in one team from being transmitted to others? Often you can't—but knowing how teams are connected through shared membership allows you to anticipate *where* some shocks may be transferred and to design small amounts of slack into the system to absorb them. This doesn't mean having people sit around twiddling their thumbs just in case. Rather, you're enabling them to shift their attention when needed. One engineering firm we worked with had identified several skilled "firefighters" and assigned them to long-term projects that wouldn't suffer if they had to address urgent problems elsewhere. This had the added benefit of providing those individuals with exciting challenges that were a welcome change of pace from their day-to-day work.

It takes a critical eye and a clear set of strategic priorities to determine which projects can be disrupted and which can't. Sometimes it makes sense to give certain projects "protected" status, exempting members of those teams from answering others' firefighting calls. Overall, the idea is to be responsive to immediate problems without sacrificing teams' ongoing needs. Of course, even if you've built slack into team design, you may occasionally have to jump in with extra resources to save critical projects that take a hit. But your other teams will feel less pain when you do.

None of this is easy. You may need to work with HR or IT to establish processes or systems that will allow you to track multiteaming more accurately across the organization. You may even need to create a new role to define and coordinate these efforts effectively. And people may resist the increased oversight—it can feel like micro-management to team leaders and members who are accustomed to having freer rein, particularly in entrepreneurial cultures. Still, in the end such investments are worthwhile; it's actually more costly to allow the trade-offs of multiteaming to go unchecked. If you're open about the problems you're trying to solve with all this transparency, people are less likely to feel surveilled or constrained by it and more likely to see the upside.

Nearly every knowledge worker these days is a member of multiple concurrent teams. Together, organizational and team leaders can make the most of that trend by creating an environment where multiteamers will thrive. Some of this involves managing inter-dependence risks, articulating and navigating groups' competing priorities, and removing obstacles to strategic coordination across groups. And some entails building stronger connections and greater trust among people who spend only a small fraction of their time together.

All around, it's a significant investment of time and effort. But organizations pay a much higher price when they neglect the costs of multiteaming in hot pursuit of its benefits.

Originally published in September–October 2017. Reprint R1705C

Global Teams
That Work

by Tsedal Neeley

TO SUCCEED IN THE GLOBAL ECONOMY TODAY, more and more companies are relying on a geographically dispersed workforce. They build teams that offer the best functional expertise from around the world, combined with deep, local knowledge of the most promising markets. They draw on the benefits of international diversity, bringing together people from many cultures with varied work experiences and different perspectives on strategic and organizational challenges. All this helps multinational companies compete in the current business environment.

But managers who actually lead global teams are up against stiff challenges. Creating successful work groups is hard enough when everyone is local and people share the same office space. But when team members come from different countries and functional backgrounds and are working in different locations, communication can rapidly deteriorate, misunderstanding can ensue, and cooperation can degenerate into distrust.

Preventing this vicious dynamic from taking place has been a focus of my research, teaching, and consulting for more than 15 years. I have conducted dozens of studies and heard from countless executives and managers about misunderstandings within the global teams they have joined or led, sometimes with costly consequences. But I have also encountered teams that have produced remarkable innovations, creating millions of dollars in value for their customers and shareholders.

One basic difference between global teams that work and those that don't lies in the level of social distance—the degree of emotional connection among team members. When people on a team all work in the same place, the level of social distance is usually low. Even if they come from different backgrounds, people can interact formally and informally, align, and build trust. They arrive at a common understanding of what certain behaviors mean, and they feel close and congenial, which fosters good teamwork. Coworkers who are geographically separated, however, can't easily connect and align, so they experience high levels of social distance and struggle to develop effective interactions. Mitigating social distance therefore becomes the primary management challenge for the global team leader.

To help in this task, I have developed and tested a framework for identifying and successfully managing social distance. It is called the SPLIT framework, reflecting its five components: structure, process, language, identity, and technology—each of which can be a source of social distance. In the following pages I explain how each can lead to team dysfunction and describe how smart leaders can fix problems that occur—or prevent them from happening in the first place.

Structure and the Perception of Power

In the context of global teams, the structural factors determining social distance are the location and number of sites where team members are based and the number of employees who work at each site.

The fundamental issue here is the perception of power. If most team members are located in Germany, for instance, with two or three in the United States and in South Africa, there may be a sense that the German members have more power. This imbalance sets up a negative dynamic. People in the larger (majority) group may feel resentment toward the minority group, believing that the latter will try to get away with contributing less than its fair share. Meanwhile,

Idea in Brief

The Problem

When teams consist of people from different cultures working apart from one another in different locations, social distance—or a lack of emotional connection—can cause miscommunication, misunderstanding, and distrust.

The Solution

The leaders of global teams can improve the workings of their groups by using the author's SPLIT framework to identify and address five sources of social distance: structure, process, language, identity, and technology.

those in the minority group may believe that the majority is usurping what little power and voice they have.

The situation is exacerbated when the leader is at the site with the most people or the one closest to company headquarters: Team members at that site tend to ignore the needs and contributions of their colleagues at other locations. This dynamic can occur even when everyone is in the same country: The five people working in, say, Beijing may have a strong allegiance to one another and a habit of shutting out their two colleagues in Shanghai.

When geographically dispersed team members perceive a power imbalance, they often come to feel that there are in-groups and out-groups. Consider the case of a global marketing team for a US-based multinational pharmaceutical company. The leader and the core strategy group for the Americas worked in the company's Boston-area headquarters. A smaller group in London and a single individual in Moscow focused on the markets in Europe. Three other team members, who split their time between Singapore and Tokyo, were responsible for strategy in Asia. The way that each group perceived its situation is illustrated in the sidebar "Views from a Dispersed Team."

To correct perceived power imbalances between different groups, a leader needs to get three key messages across:

Who we are

The team is a single entity, even though individual members may be very different from one another. The leader should encourage sensitivity to differences but look for ways to bridge them and build unity.

Views from a Dispersed Team

THE MARKETING TEAM of a multinational pharmaceutical company had 17 members in different locations. Each group, depending on size and proximity to the leader in Boston, saw the power structure differently.

Moscow, 1 person
"I am all on my own here and at the mercy of the Boston group. I need to make sure that the boss has my back."

Singapore/Tokyo, 3 people
"Our opinions are often ignored. It's so difficult to find a good time to exchange ideas, and even if we do manage to connect, we can't get a word in edgewise."

London, 5 people
"We represent the most challenging regions in terms of diversity and institutional hurdles. The Boston team really doesn't understand our markets."

Boston, 8 people
"We do the important work and have easy access to the boss."

Tariq, a 33-year-old rising star in a global firm, was assigned to lead a 68-person division whose members hailed from 27 countries, spoke 18 languages, and ranged in age from 22 to 61. During the two years before he took charge, the group's performance had been in a precipitous decline and employee satisfaction had plunged. Tariq saw that the team had fractured into subgroups according to location and language. To bring people back together, he introduced a team motto ("We are different yet one"), created opportunities for employees to talk about their cultures, and instituted a zero-tolerance policy for displays of cultural insensitivity.

What we do
It's important to remind team members that they share a common purpose and to direct their energy toward business-unit or corporate goals. The leader should periodically highlight how everyone's work fits into the company's overall strategy and advances its position in the market. For instance, during a weekly conference call, a global team leader might review the group's performance relative to

company objectives. She might also discuss the level of collective focus and sharpness the team needs in order to fend off competitors.

I am there for you

Team members located far from the leader require frequent contact with him or her. A brief phone call or e-mail can make all the difference in conveying that their contributions matter. For instance, one manager in Dallas, Texas, inherited a large group in India as part of an acquisition. He made it a point to involve those employees in important decisions, contact them frequently to discuss ongoing projects, and thank them for good work. He even called team members personally to give them their birthdays off. His team appreciated his attention and became more cohesive as a result.

Process and the Importance of Empathy

It almost goes without saying that empathy helps reduce social distance. If colleagues can talk informally around a watercooler—whether about work or about personal matters—they are more likely to develop an empathy that helps them interact productively in more-formal contexts. Because geographically dispersed team members lack regular face time, they are less likely to have a sense of mutual understanding. To foster this, global team leaders need to make sure they build the following "deliberate moments" into the process for meeting virtually:

Feedback on routine interactions

Members of global teams may unwittingly send the wrong signals with their everyday behavior. Julie, a French chemical engineer, and her teammates in Marseille checked and responded to e-mails only first thing in the morning, to ensure an uninterrupted workday. They had no idea that this practice was routinely adding an overnight delay to correspondence with their American colleagues and contributing to mistrust. It was not until Julie visited the team's offices in California that the French group realized there was a problem. Of course, face-to-face visits are not the only way to acquire such learning. Remote team members can also use the phone, e-mail, or even videoconferencing to check in with one another and ask how the collaboration is going. The point is that leaders and members of global teams must actively elicit this kind of "reflected knowledge," or awareness of how others see them.

Unstructured time

Think back to your last face-to-face meeting. During the first few minutes before the official discussion began, what was the atmosphere like? Were people comparing notes on the weather, their kids, that new restaurant in town? Unstructured communication like this is positive, because it allows for the organic unfolding of processes that must occur in all business dealings—sharing knowledge, coordinating and monitoring interactions, and building relationships. Even when people are spread all over the world, small talk is still a powerful way to promote trust. So when planning your team's call-in meetings, factor in five minutes for light conversation before business gets under way. Especially during the first meetings, take the lead in initiating informal discussions about work and nonwork matters that allow team members to get to know their distant counterparts. In particular, encourage people to be open about constraints they face outside the project, even if those aren't directly linked to the matter at hand.

Time to disagree

Leaders should encourage disagreement both about the team's tasks and about the process by which the tasks get done. The challenge, of course, is to take the heat out of the debate. Framing meetings as brainstorming opportunities lowers the risk that people will feel pressed to choose between sides. Instead, they will see an invitation to evaluate agenda items and contribute their ideas. As the leader, model the act of questioning to get to the heart of things. Solicit each team member's views on each topic you discuss, starting with those who have the least status or experience with the group so that they don't feel intimidated by others' comments. This may initially seem like a waste of time, but if you seek opinions up front, you may make better decisions and get buy-in from more people.

A software developer in Istanbul kept silent in a team meeting in order to avoid conflict, even though he questioned his colleagues' design of a particular feature. He had good reasons to oppose their decision, but his team leader did not brook disagreement, and the developer did not want to damage his own position. However, four weeks into the project, the team ran into the very problems that the developer had seen coming.

Language and the Fluency Gap

Good communication among coworkers drives effective knowledge sharing, decision making, coordination, and, ultimately, performance results (see also "What's Your Language Strategy?" by Tsedal Neeley and Robert Steven Kaplan, HBR, September 2014). But in global teams, varying levels of fluency with the chosen common language are inevitable—and likely to heighten social distance. The team members who can communicate best in the organization's lingua franca (usually English) often exert the most influence, while those who are less fluent often become inhibited and withdraw. Mitigating these effects typically involves insisting that all team members respect three rules for communicating in meetings:

Dial down dominance
Strong speakers must agree to slow down their speaking pace and use fewer idioms, slang terms, and esoteric cultural references when addressing the group. They should limit the number of comments they make within a set time frame, depending on the pace of the meeting and the subject matter. They should actively seek confirmation that they've been understood, and they should practice active listening by rephrasing others' statements for clarification or emphasis.

Dial up engagement
Less fluent speakers should monitor the frequency of their responses in meetings to ensure that they are contributing. In some cases, it's even worth asking them to set goals for the number of comments

they make within a given period. Don't let them use their own language and have a teammate translate, because that can alienate others. As with fluent speakers, team members who are less proficient in the language must always confirm that they have been understood. Encourage them to routinely ask if others are following them. Similarly, when listening, they should be empowered to say they have not understood something. It can be tough for nonnative speakers to make this leap, yet doing so keeps them from being marginalized.

Balance participation to ensure inclusion

Getting commitments to good speaking behavior is the easy part; making the behavior happen will require active management. Global team leaders must keep track of who is and isn't contributing and deliberately solicit participation from less fluent speakers. Sometimes it may also be necessary to get dominant-language speakers to dial down to ensure that the proposals and perspectives of less fluent speakers are heard.

The leader of a global team based in Dubai required all his reports to post the three communication rules in their cubicles. Soon he noted that one heavily accented European team member began contributing to discussions for the first time since joining the group 17 months earlier. The rules had given this person the license, opportunity, and responsibility to speak up. As a leader, you could try the same tactics with your own team, distributing copies of the sidebar "Rules of Engagement for Team Meetings."

Identity and the Mismatch of Perceptions

Global teams work most smoothly when members "get" where their colleagues are coming from. However, deciphering someone's identity and finding ways to relate is far from simple. People define themselves in terms of a multitude of variables—age, gender, nationality, ethnicity, religion, occupation, political ties, and so forth. And although behavior can be revealing, particular behaviors may signify different things depending on the individual's identity. For example, someone in North America who looks you squarely in

Rules of Engagement for Team Meetings

ALL TEAM MEMBERS should be guided by these three rules to ensure that influence on decisions is not dictated by fluency in the company's lingua franca.

Fluent speakers: Dial down dominance	Slow down the pace and use familiar language (e.g., fewer idioms). Refrain from dominating the conversation. Ask: "Do you understand what I am saying?" Listen actively.
Less fluent speakers: Dial up engagement	Resist withdrawal or other avoidance behaviors. Refrain from reverting to your native language. Ask: "Do you understand what I am saying?" If you don't understand others, ask them to repeat or explain.
Team leaders: Balance for inclusion	Monitor participants and strive to balance their speaking and listening. Actively draw contributions from all team members. Solicit participation from less fluent speakers in particular. Be prepared to define and interpret content.

the eye may project confidence and honesty, but in other parts of the world, direct eye contact might be perceived as rude or threatening. Misunderstandings such as this are a major source of social distance and distrust, and global team leaders have to raise everyone's awareness of them. This involves mutual learning and teaching.

Learning from one another

When adapting to a new cultural environment, a savvy leader will avoid making assumptions about what behaviors mean. Take a step back, watch, and listen. In America, someone who says, "Yes, I can do this" likely means she is willing and able to do what you asked. In India, however, the same statement may simply signal that she wants to try—not that she's confident of success. Before drawing conclusions, therefore, ask a lot of questions. In the example just described, you might probe to see if the team member anticipates any challenges or needs additional resources. Asking for this information may yield greater insight into how the person truly feels about accomplishing the task.

The give-and-take of asking questions and providing answers establishes two-way communication between the leader and team members. And if a leader regularly solicits input, acting as a student rather than an expert with hidden knowledge, he empowers others on the team, leading them to participate more willingly and effectively. A non-Mandarin-speaking manager in China relied heavily on his local staff during meetings with clients in order to better understand clients' perceptions of the interactions and to gauge the appropriateness of his own behavior. His team members began to see themselves as essential to the development of client relationships and felt valued, which motivated them to perform at even higher levels.

In this model, everyone is a teacher and a learner, which enables people to step out of their traditional roles. Team members take on more responsibility for the development of the team as a whole. Leaders learn to see themselves as unfinished and are thus more likely to adjust their style to reflect the team's needs. They instruct but they also facilitate, helping team members to parse their observations and understand one another's true identities.

A case in point

Consider the experience of Daniel, the leader of a recently formed multinational team spread over four continents. During a conference call, he asked people to discuss a particular strategy for reaching a new market in a challenging location. This was the first time he had raised a topic on which there was a range of opinion.

Daniel observed that Theo, a member of the Israeli team, regularly interrupted Angela, a member of the Buenos Aires team, and their ideas were at odds. Although tempted to jump in and play referee, Daniel held back. To his surprise, neither Theo nor Angela got frustrated. They went back and forth, bolstering their positions by referencing typical business practices and outcomes in their respective countries, but they stayed committed to reaching a group consensus.

At the meeting's end, Daniel shared his observations with the team, addressing not only the content of the discussion, but also the manner in which it took place. "Theo and Angela," he said, "when you began to hash out your ideas, I was concerned that both of you might have felt you weren't being heard or weren't getting a chance to fully express your thoughts. But now you both seem satisfied that you were able to make your arguments, articulate cultural perspectives, and help us decide on our next steps. Is that true?"

Theo and Angela affirmed Daniel's observations and provided an additional contextual detail: Six months earlier they had worked together on another project—an experience that allowed them to establish their own style of relating to each other. Their ability to acknowledge and navigate their cultural differences was beneficial to everyone on the team. Not only did it help move their work forward, but it showed that conflict does not have to create social distance. And Daniel gained more information about Theo and Angela, which would help him manage the team more effectively in the future.

Technology and the Connection Challenge

The modes of communication used by global teams must be carefully considered, because the technologies can both reduce and increase social distance. Videoconferencing, for instance, allows rich communication in which both context and emotion can be perceived. E-mail offers greater ease and efficiency but lacks contextual cues. In making decisions about which technology to use, a leader must ask the following:

Should communication be instant?

Teleconferencing and videoconferencing enable real-time (instant) conversations. E-mail and certain social media formats require users to wait for the other party to respond. Choosing between instant and delayed forms of communication can be especially challenging for global teams. For example, when a team spans multiple time zones, a telephone call may not be convenient for everyone. The Japanese team leader of a US-based multinational put it this way: "I have three or four days per week when I have a conference call with global executives. In most cases, it starts at 9:00 or 10:00 in the night. If we can take the conference call in the daytime, it's much easier for me. But we are in the Far East, and headquarters is in the United States, so we have to make the best of it."

Instant technologies are valuable when leaders need to persuade others to adopt their viewpoint. But if they simply want to share information, then delayed methods such as e-mail are simpler, more efficient, and less disruptive to people's lives. Leaders must also consider the team's interpersonal dynamics. If the team has a history of conflict, technology choices that limit the opportunities for real-time emotional exchanges may yield the best results.

In general, the evidence suggests that most companies overrely on delayed communication. A recent Forrester survey of nearly 10,000 information workers in 17 countries showed that 94% of employees report using e-mail, but only 33% ever participate in desktop videoconferencing (with apps such as Skype and Viber), and a mere 25% use room-based videoconferencing. These numbers will surely change over time, as the tools evolve and users become more comfortable with them, but leaders need to choose their format carefully: instant or delayed.

Do I need to reinforce the message?

Savvy leaders will communicate through multiple platforms to ensure that messages are understood and remembered. For example, if a manager electronically assigns one of her team members a task by entering notes into a daily work log, she may then follow up with a text or a face-to-face chat to ensure that the team member saw the request and recognized its urgency.

Redundant communication is also effective for leaders who are concerned about convincing others that their message is important. Greg, for instance, a project manager in a medical devices organization, found that his team was falling behind on the development of a product. He called an emergency meeting to discuss the issues and explain new corporate protocols for releasing new products, which he felt would bring the project back on track.

During this initial meeting, he listened to people's concerns and addressed their questions in real time. Although he felt he had communicated his position clearly and obtained the necessary verbal buy-in, he followed up the meeting by sending a carefully drafted e-mail to all the attendees, reiterating the agreed-upon changes and asking for everyone's electronic sign-off. This redundant communication helped reinforce acceptance of his ideas and increased the likelihood that his colleagues would actually implement the new protocols.

Am I leading by example?

Team members very quickly pick up on the leader's personal preferences regarding communication technology. A leader who wants to encourage people to videoconference should communicate this way herself. If she wants employees to pick up the phone and speak to one another, she had better be a frequent user of the phone. And if she wants team members to respond quickly to e-mails, she needs to set the example.

Flexibility and appreciation for diversity are at the heart of managing a global team. Leaders must expect problems and patterns to change or repeat themselves as teams shift, disband, and regroup. But there is at least one constant: To manage social distance effectively and maximize the talents and engagement of team members, leaders must stay attentive to all five of the SPLIT dimensions. Decisions about *structure* create opportunities for good *process*, which can mitigate difficulties caused by *language* differences and *identity* issues. If leaders act on these fronts, while marshaling *technology* to improve communication among geographically dispersed colleagues, social distance is sure to shrink, not expand. When that happens, teams can become truly representative of the "global village"—not just because of their international makeup, but also because their members feel mutual trust and a sense of kinship. They can then embrace and practice the kind of innovative, respectful, and groundbreaking interactions that drive the best ideas forward.

Originally published in October 2015. Reprint R1510D

Creating the Best Workplace on Earth

by Rob Goffee and Gareth Jones

SUPPOSE YOU WANT TO DESIGN the best company on earth to work for. What would it be like? For three years we've been investigating this question by asking hundreds of executives in surveys and in seminars all over the world to describe their ideal organization. This mission arose from our research into the relationship between authenticity and effective leadership. Simply put, people will not follow a leader they feel is inauthentic. But the executives we questioned made it clear that to be authentic, they needed to work for an authentic organization.

What did they mean? Many of their answers were highly specific, of course. But underlying the differences of circumstance, industry, and individual ambition we found six common imperatives. Together they describe an organization that operates at its fullest potential by allowing people to do their best work.

We call this "the organization of your dreams." In a nutshell, it's a company where individual differences are nurtured; information is not suppressed or spun; the company adds value to employees, rather than merely extracting it from them; the organization stands for something meaningful; the work itself is intrinsically rewarding; and there are no stupid rules.

These principles might all sound commonsensical. Who wouldn't want to work in a place that follows them? Executives are certainly aware of the benefits, which many studies have confirmed. Take these two examples: Research from the Hay Group finds that highly engaged employees are, on average, 50% more likely to exceed expectations than the least-engaged workers. And companies with highly engaged people outperform firms with the most disengaged folks—by 54% in employee retention, by 89% in customer satisfaction, and by fourfold in revenue growth. Recent research by our London Business School colleague Dan Cable shows that employees who feel welcome to express their authentic selves at work exhibit higher levels of organizational commitment, individual performance, and propensity to help others.

Yet, few, if any, organizations possess all six virtues. Several of the attributes run counter to traditional practices and ingrained habits. Others are, frankly, complicated and can be costly to implement. Some conflict with one another. Almost all require leaders to carefully balance competing interests and to rethink how they allocate their time and attention.

So the company of your dreams remains largely aspirational. We offer our findings, therefore, as a challenge: an agenda for leaders and organizations that aim to create the most productive and rewarding working environment possible.

Let People Be Themselves

When companies try to accommodate differences, they too often confine themselves to traditional diversity categories—gender, race, age, ethnicity, and the like. These efforts are laudable, but the executives we interviewed were after something more subtle—differences in perspectives, habits of mind, and core assumptions.

The vice chancellor at one of the world's leading universities, for instance, would walk around campus late at night to locate the research hot spots. A tough-minded physicist, he expected to find them in the science labs. But much to his surprise, he discovered them in all kinds of academic disciplines—ancient history, drama, the Spanish department.

Idea in Brief

You want to design the best company on earth to work for. What would it be like? The response from hundreds of executives all over the world, in a nutshell, is that their dream organization is a place where:

- You can be yourself.
- You're told what's really going on.
- Your strengths are magnified.
- The company stands for something meaningful.
- Your daily work is rewarding.
- Stupid rules don't exist.

Those virtues seem like common sense, but few companies exemplify all six. Some of the attributes conflict, and many are complicated, costly, or time-consuming to implement. Almost all of them require leaders to carefully balance competing interests and reallocate their time and attention. So the list stands as a challenge: It's an agenda for executives who aim to create the most productive and rewarding working environment possible.

The ideal organization is aware of dominant currents in its culture, work habits, dress code, traditions, and governing assumptions but, like the chancellor, makes explicit efforts to transcend them. We are talking not just about the buttoned-down financial services company that embraces the IT guys in shorts and sandals, but also the hipster organization that doesn't look askance when someone wears a suit. Or the place where nearly everyone comes in at odd hours but that accommodates the one or two people who prefer a 9-to-5 schedule.

For example, at LVMH, the world's largest luxury-goods company (and growing rapidly), you'd expect to find brilliant, creative innovators like Marc Jacobs and Phoebe Philo. And you do. But alongside them you also encounter a higher-than-expected proportion of executives and specialists who monitor and assess ideas with an analytical business focus. One of the ingredients in LVMH's success is having a culture where opposite types can thrive and work cooperatively. Careful selection is part of the secret: LVMH looks for creative people who want their designs to be marketable and who, in turn, are more likely to appreciate monitors who are skilled at spotting commercial potential.

The benefits of tapping the full range of people's knowledge and talents may be obvious, yet it's not surprising that so few companies do it. For one thing, uncovering biases isn't easy. (Consider the assumption the diligent chancellor made when he equated research intensity with late-night lab work.) More fundamentally, though, efforts to nurture individuality run up against countervailing efforts to increase organizational effectiveness by forging clear incentive systems and career paths. Competence models, appraisal systems, management by objectives, and tightly defined recruitment policies all narrow the range of acceptable behavior.

Companies that succeed in nurturing individuality, therefore, may have to forgo some degree of organizational orderliness. Take Arup, perhaps the world's most creative engineering and design company. Many iconic buildings bear the mark of Arup's distinctive imprint—from the Sydney Opera House to the Centre Pompidou to the Beijing Water Cube.

Arup approaches its work holistically. When the firm builds a suspension bridge, for example, it looks beyond the concerns of the immediate client to the region that relies on the bridge. To do so, Arup's people collaborate with mathematicians, economists, artists, and politicians alike. Accordingly, Arup considers the capacity to absorb different skill sets and personalities as key to its strategy. "We want there to be interesting parts that don't quite fit in . . . that take us places where we didn't expect to get to," says chairman Philip Dilley. "That's part of my job now—to prevent it from becoming totally orderly."

Conventional appraisal systems don't work in such a world, so Arup doesn't use quantitative performance-measurement systems or articulate a corporate policy on how employees should progress. Managers make their expectations clear, but individuals decide how to meet them. "Self-determination means setting your own path and being accountable for your success," a senior HR official explains. "Development and progression is your own business, with our support."

If this sounds too chaotic for a more conventional company, consider Waitrose, one of Britain's most successful food retailers, according to measures as diverse as market share, profitability, and customer and staff loyalty. In an industry that necessarily focuses on executing processes efficiently, Waitrose sees its competitive edge in nurturing the small sparks of creativity that make a big difference to the customer experience.

Waitrose is a cooperative: Every employee is a co-owner who shares in the company's annual profits. So the source of staff loyalty is not much of a mystery. But even so, the company goes to great lengths to draw out and support people's personal interests. If you want to learn piano, Waitrose will pay half the cost of the lessons. There's a thriving club culture—cooking, crafts, swimming, and so on. We have a friend whose father learned to sail because he worked for this organization. In that way, Waitrose strives to create an atmosphere where people feel comfortable being themselves. We were struck when a senior executive told us, "Friends and family would recognize me at work."

"Great retail businesses depend on characters who do things a bit differently," another executive explained. "Over the years we have had lots of them. We must be careful to cherish them and make sure our systems don't squeeze them out."

Pursuit of predictability leads to a culture of conformity, what Émile Durkheim called "mechanical solidarity." But companies like LVMH, Arup, and Waitrose are forged out of "organic solidarity"—which, Durkheim argued, rests on the productive exploitation of differences. Why go to all the trouble? We think Ted Mathas, head of the mutual insurance company New York Life, explains it best: "When I was appointed CEO, my biggest concern was, would this [job] allow me to truly say what I think? I needed to be myself to do a good job. Everybody does."

Unleash the Flow of Information

The organization of your dreams does not deceive, stonewall, distort, or spin. It recognizes that in the age of Facebook, WikiLeaks, and Twitter, you're better off telling people the truth before someone else does. It respects its employees' need to know what's really going on

The "Dream Company" Diagnostic

HOW CLOSE IS YOUR ORGANIZATION to the ideal? To find out, check off each statement that applies. The more checkmarks you have, the closer you are to the dream.

Let Me Be Myself

- ☐ I'm the same person at home as I am at work.
- ☐ I feel comfortable being myself.
- ☐ We're all encouraged to express our differences.
- ☐ People who think differently from most do well here.
- ☐ Passion is encouraged, even when it leads to conflict.
- ☐ More than one type of person fits in here.

Tell Me What's Really Going On

- ☐ We're all told the whole story.
- ☐ Information is not spun.
- ☐ It's not disloyal to say something negative.
- ☐ My manager wants to hear bad news.
- ☐ Top executives want to hear bad news.
- ☐ Many channels of communication are available to us.
- ☐ I feel comfortable signing my name to comments I make.

Discover and Magnify My Strengths

- ☐ I am given the chance to develop.
- ☐ Every employee is given the chance to develop.
- ☐ The best people want to strut their stuff here.
- ☐ The weakest performers can see a path to improvement.
- ☐ Compensation is fairly distributed throughout the organization.

---

so that they can do their jobs, particularly in volatile environments where it's already difficult to keep everyone aligned and where workers at all levels are being asked to think more strategically. You'd imagine that would be self-evident to managers everywhere. In reality, the

☐ We generate value for ourselves by adding value to others.

Make Me Proud I Work Here

☐ I know what we stand for.

☐ I value what we stand for.

☐ I want to exceed my current duties.

☐ Profit is not our overriding goal.

☐ I am accomplishing something worthwhile.

☐ I like to tell people where I work.

Make My Work Meaningful

☐ My job is meaningful to me.

☐ My duties make sense to me.

☐ My work gives me energy and pleasure.

☐ I understand how my job fits with everyone else's.

☐ Everyone's job is necessary.

☐ At work we share a common cause.

Don't Hinder Me with Stupid Rules

☐ We keep things simple.

☐ The rules are clear and apply equally to everyone.

☐ I know what the rules are for.

☐ Everyone knows what the rules are for.

☐ We, as an organization, resist red tape.

☐ Authority is respected.

barriers to what we call "radical honesty"—that is, entirely candid, complete, clear, and timely communication—are legion.

Some managers see parceling out information on a need-to-know basis as important to maintaining efficiency. Others practice a seemingly benign type of paternalism, reluctant to worry staff with certain information or to identify a problem before having a solution. Some feel an obligation to put a positive spin on even the most negative situations out of a best-foot-forward sense of loyalty to the organization.

The reluctance to be the bearer of bad news is deeply human, and many top executives well know that this tendency can strangle the flow of critical information. Take Novo Nordisk's Mads Øvlisen, who was CEO in the 1990s, when violations of FDA regulations at the company's Danish insulin-production facilities became so serious that US regulators nearly banned the insulin from the US market. Incredible as it seems in hindsight, no one told Øvlisen about the situation. That's because Novo Nordisk operated under a culture in which the executive management board was never supposed to receive bad news.

The company took formal steps to rectify the situation, redesigning the company's entire quality-management system—its processes, procedures, and training of all involved personnel. Eventually, those practices were extended to new-product development, manufacturing, distribution, sales, and support systems. More generally, a vision, core values, and a set of management principles were explicitly articulated as the Novo Nordisk Way. To get at the root cause of the crisis, Øvlisen also set out to create a new culture of honesty through a process he called "organizational facilitation"— that is, facilitation of the flow of honest information.

A core team of facilitators (internal management auditors) with long organizational experience now regularly visit all of the company's worldwide affiliates. They interview randomly selected employees and managers to assess whether the Novo Nordisk Way is being practiced. Employees know, for instance, that they must inform all stakeholders both within and outside the organization of what's happening, even when something goes wrong, as quickly as possible. Does this really happen? Many employees have told us that they appreciate these site visits because they foster honest conversations about fundamental business values and processes.

Radical honesty is not easy to implement. It requires opening many different communication channels, which can be time-consuming to maintain. And for previously insulated top managers, it can be somewhat ego-bruising. Witness what ensued when Novo Nordisk recently banned soda from all its buildings. PeopleCom, the company's internal news site, was flooded with hundreds of passionate responses. Some people saw it as an attack on personal freedom. ("I wonder what will be the next thing NN will 'help' me not to do," wrote one exasperated employee. "Ban fresh fruit in an effort to reduce sugar consumption?") Others defended the policy as a logical extension of the company's focus on diabetes. ("We can still purchase our own sugary soft drinks . . . Novo Nordisk shouldn't be a 7-Eleven.") That all these comments were signed indicates how much honesty has infused Novo Nordisk's culture.

Trade secrets will always require confidentiality. And we don't want to suggest that honesty will necessarily stop problems from arising, particularly in highly regulated industries that routinely find themselves under scrutiny. We maintain, though, that executives should err on the side of transparency far more than their instincts suggest. Particularly today, when trust levels among both employees and customers are so low and background noise is so high, organizations must work very hard to communicate what's going on if they are to be heard and believed.

Magnify People's Strengths

The ideal company makes its best employees even better—and the least of them better than they ever thought they could be. In robust economies, when competition for talent is fierce, it's easy to see that the benefits of developing existing staff outweigh the costs of finding new workers. But even then, companies grumble about losing their investment when people decamp for more-promising opportunities. In both good times and bad, managers are far more often rewarded for minimizing labor costs than for the longer-term goal of increasing workers' effectiveness. Perhaps that explains why this aspiration, while so widely recognized and well understood, often remains unfulfilled.

Elite universities and hospitals, Goldman Sachs and McKinsey, and design firms like Arup have all been adding value to valuable people for a very long time. Google and Apple are more recent examples. They do this in myriad ways—by providing networks, creative interaction with peers, stretch assignments, training, and a brand that confers elite status on employees. None of this is rocket science, nor is it likely to be news to anyone.

But the challenge of finding, training, and retaining excellent workers is not confined to specialized, high-tech, or high-finance industries. We contend that the employee-employer relationship is shifting in many industries from how much value can be extracted from workers to how much can be instilled in them. At heart, that's what productivity improvement really means.

Take McDonald's, a company founded on the primacy of cost efficiency. In an economy with plenty of people looking for jobs, McDonald's nevertheless focuses on the growth paths of its front-line workers—and on a large scale. In the UK, the company invests £36 million ($55 million) a year in giving its 87,500 employees the chance to gain a wide range of nationally recognized academic qualifications while they work. One of the largest apprenticeship providers in the country, McDonald's has awarded more than 35,000 such qualifications to employees since the program's launch in 2006. Every week the equivalent of six full classes of students acquire formal credentials in math and English. Every day another 20 employees earn an apprenticeship qualification.

Like many large companies, McDonald's has extensive management training programs for its executives, but the firm also extends that effort to restaurant general managers, department managers, and shift managers who, as the day-to-day leaders on the front lines, are taught the communication and coaching skills they need to motivate crews and to hit their shifts' sales targets. The return on the company's investment is measured not in terms of increased revenue or profitability but in lower turnover of hourly managers and their crews. Turnover has declined steadily since the programs were initiated, as reflected in the Great Place to Work Institute's recognition of McDonald's as one of the 50 best workplaces every year since 2007.

To get a sense of how far employee development can be taken, consider Games Makers, the volunteer training effort mounted by the London Organising Committee of the Olympic Games. LOCOG was responsible for the largest peacetime workforce ever assembled in the UK. It coordinated the activities of more than 100,000 subcontractors, 70,000 Games Makers volunteers, and 8,000 paid staff. Games Makers used bold, imaginative schemes to employ people who had never worked or volunteered before. Through its Trailblazer program, for example, paid staff learned how to work effectively with volunteers of all social backgrounds. Through a partnership with other state agencies, the Personal Best program enabled more than 7,500 disadvantaged, long-term-unemployed individuals, some with physical or learning disabilities, to earn a job qualification. Games Makers' School Leavers program targeted students who have left school in east London, the host borough for the games, by granting them two three-month placements that, upon successful completion, were followed by a contract for employment until the end of the event. LOCOG's model has inspired government agencies and private-sector employment bureaus in the UK to rewrite their work-engagement guidelines to enable them to tap into—and make productive—a far wider range of people than had previously been considered employable.

We recognize that promising to bring out the best in everyone is a high-risk, high-reward strategy. It raises reputational capital, and such capital is easily destroyed. Goldman Sachs, for one, spent years building its reputation as the most exciting investment bank of all. That's why Greg Smith's scathing resignation letter, accusing the company of not living up to its own standards, was so damaging. Once a company heads down this road, it has to keep going.

Stand for More Than Shareholder Value

People want to be a part of something bigger than themselves, something they can believe in. "I've worked in organizations where people try to brainwash me about the virtues of the brand," one seminar participant told us. "I want to work in an organization where I can really feel where the company comes from and what it stands for so that I can live the brand."

It has become commonplace to assert that organizations need shared meaning, and this is surely so. But shared meaning is about more than fulfilling your mission statement—it's about forging and maintaining powerful connections between personal and organizational values. When you do that, you foster individuality and a strong culture at the same time.

Some people might argue that certain companies have an inherent advantage in this area. An academic colleague once asked us if we were working with anyone interesting. When we mentioned Novo Nordisk, he produced from his briefcase a set of Novo pens for injecting insulin and said simply, "They save my life every day." Engineers who design the side bars for BMW's mini have been known to wake up at 4:00 in the morning to write down ideas that will make the cars safer. And that might be expected of people drawn to the idea of building "the ultimate driving machine."

But the advantage these companies have is not the businesses they're in. The connections they forge stem, rather, from the way they do business. To understand how that works more generally, consider Michael Barry, who once was a teacher made redundant by state spending cuts. Three decades later, the experience remained vividly traumatic: "It was a case of 'last in, first out,' nothing to do with merit. I decided I never wanted to lose my job like that again. I researched things quite carefully, looking for places that were clear about what they wanted."

And where did this idealistic man go? He became an insurance salesman for New York Life. "It is a very different company—from the top down," he said, when we asked him what connection he felt to the company. He further explained it this way: "Back when other life insurance companies were demutualizing and becoming financial services supermarkets, New York Life made it very clear that life insurance would remain our core focus. The agents didn't like it [at first]—they felt they were losing the opportunity to make more money. But Sy Sternberg, the CEO at that time, went to public forums with the agents and pulled no punches. He told us, 'We are a life insurance company, and we are good at it.'" This is more than a business strategy, Barry says. "It's how we operate every day. This is not a place where we wriggle out of claims. One man took out a life policy, went home to write out the check. It was on his desk when he died that night. The policy was unpaid, but we paid the claim. The agents really buy into this."

Current CEO Ted Mathas acknowledges that New York Life's status as a mutual company gives it an advantage in claiming that profit is not all that matters. But he argues that the same logic applies for public firms—that profit is (or should be) an outcome of the pursuit of other, more meaningful goals. Again, this is hardly a new idea. "But many companies in public ownership have lost their way and with it a sense of who they are," Mathas suggests, and we agree.

Show How the Daily Work Makes Sense

Beyond shared meaning, the executives we've spoken to want something else. They seek to derive meaning from their daily activities.

This aspiration cannot be fulfilled in any comprehensive way through job enrichment add-on. It requires nothing less than a deliberate reconsideration of the tasks each person is performing. Do those duties make sense? Why are they what they are? Are they as engaging as they can be? This is a huge, complex undertaking.

Take John Lewis, the parent company of Waitrose and the department store Peter Jones. In 2012 it completed a review of its more than 2,200 jobs, slotting them within a hierarchy of 10 levels, to make it easier for employees to take advantage of opportunities across the organization. This sounds like a homogenizing move, and it might be at a traditional company. But at John Lewis, which operates for the benefit of its employee owners, it was a deliberate effort to match its people with the work they want to do.

Or consider Rabobank Nederland, the banking arm of the largest financial services provider in the Netherlands, Rabobank Group. After several years of development, the bank has rolled out Rabo Unplugged, an organizational and technical infrastructure that allows employees to connect to one another from practically anywhere while still meeting the stringent encryption standards that banking systems require. With no fixed offices or rigid job descriptions, Rabobank's employees are, like Arup's, responsible for the results of their work. But they are free to choose how, where, when, and with whom to carry it out. This approach requires managers to place an extraordinary amount of trust in subordinates, and it demands that employees become more entrepreneurial and collaborative.

Beyond reconsidering individual roles, making work rewarding may mean rethinking the way companies are led. Arup's organization, which might be described as "extreme seamless," is one possible model. As such, it takes some getting used to. In describing how this works in Arup's Associates unit, board member Tristram Carfrae explains: "We have architects, engineers, quantity surveyors, and project managers in the same room together . . . people who genuinely want to submerge their own egos into the collective and not [be led] in the classic sense." That was a challenge for Carfrae, who as a structural engineer wrestled with the question of when to impose his will on the team and push it toward a structural, rather than a mechanical or an architecturally oriented, solution. To participate in such an evenhanded, interdependent environment is extremely hard, he says. There were "incredible rewards when it worked well and incredible frustrations when it didn't."

We don't wish to underplay this challenge. But we suggest that the benefits of rising to it are potentially very great. Where work is meaningful, it typically becomes a cause, as it is for the engineers at BMW and the agents at New York Life. We also acknowledge an element of risk: When we interviewed legendary games designer Will Wright, he told us that his primary loyalty was not to his company, Electronic Arts, but to the project—originally for him the record-breaking Sims franchise and, more recently, Spore. Wright ultimately left EA to start his own company, in which EA became a joint investor.

The challenge is similar to that of fostering personal growth. If you don't do it, the best people may leave or never consider you at all. Or your competitors may develop the potential in people you've overlooked. When you do make the investment, your staff members become more valuable to you and your competitors alike. The trick, then, is to make it meaningful for them to stay.

Have Rules People Can Believe In

No one should be surprised that, for many people, the dream organization is free of arbitrary restrictions. But it does not obliterate all rules. Engineers, even at Arup, must follow procedures and tight quality controls—or buildings will collapse.

Organizations need structure. Markets and enterprises need rules. As successful entrepreneurial businesses grow, they often come to believe that new, complicated processes will undermine their culture. But systematization need not lead to bureaucratization, not if people understand what the rules are for and view them as legitimate. Take Vestergaard Frandsen, a startup social enterprise that makes mosquito netting for the developing world. The company is mastering the art of behavior codes that can help structure its growing operations without jeopardizing its culture. Hiring (and firing) decisions are intentionally simple—only one level of approval is required for each position. Regional directors have significant freedom within clear deadlines and top- and bottom-line targets. Knowledge-management systems are designed to encourage people to call rather than e-mail one another and to explain why someone is being cc'ed on an e-mail message. Vestergaard sees these simple rules as safeguards rather than threats to its founding values.

Despite the flattening of hierarchies, the ensuing breakdown of organizational boundaries, and the unpredictability of careers, institutions remain what Max Weber calls "imperatively coordinated associations," where respect for authority is crucial for building and maintaining structure. However, we know that, increasingly, employees are skeptical of purely hierarchical power—of fancy job titles and traditional sources of legitimacy such as age and seniority. And they are becoming more suspicious of charisma, as many charismatic leaders turn out to have feet of clay.

What workers need is a sense of moral authority, derived not from a focus on the efficiency of means but from the importance of the ends they produce. The organization of your dreams gives you powerful reasons to submit to its necessary structures that support the organization's purpose. In that company, leaders' authority derives from the answer to a question that Steve Varley, managing partner of Ernst & Young UK, put to senior partners in his inaugural address, after he reported record profits and partners' earnings: "Is that all there is?" (In reply, he proposed a radical new direction—a program called "Growing Successfully, Making the Difference"— aimed at achieving both financial growth and social change.) During the past 30 years we have heard the following kinds of conversations at many organizations: "I'll be home late. I'm working on a cure for migraine." "Still at work. The new U2 album comes out tomorrow— it's brilliant." "Very busy on the plan to take insulin into East Africa." We have never heard this: "I'll be home late. I'm increasing shareholder value."

People want to do good work—to feel they matter in an organization that makes a difference. They want to work in a place that magnifies their strengths, not their weaknesses. For that, they need some autonomy and structure, and the organization must be coherent, honest, and open.

But that's tricky because it requires balancing many competing claims. Achieving the full benefit of diversity means trading the comfort of being surrounded by kindred spirits for the hard work of fitting various kinds of people, work habits, and thought traditions into a vibrant culture. Managers must continually work out when to forge ahead and when to take the time to discuss and compromise.

Our aim here is not to critique modern business structures. But it's hard not to notice that many of the organizations we've highlighted are unusual in their ownership arrangements and ambitions. Featured strongly are partnerships, mutual associations, charitable trusts, and social enterprises. Although all share a desire to generate revenue, few are conventional, large-scale capitalist enterprises.

It would be a mistake to suggest that the organizations are all alike, but two commonalities stand out. First, the institutions are all very clear about what they do well: Novo Nordisk transforms the lives of people with diabetes; Arup creates beautiful environments. Second, the organizations are suspicious, in almost a contrarian way, of fads and fashions that sweep the corporate world.

Work can be liberating, or it can be alienating, exploitative, controlling, and homogenizing. Despite the changes that new technologies and new generations bring, the underlying forces of shareholder capitalism and unexamined bureaucracy remain powerful. As you strive to create an authentic organization and fully realize human potential at work, do not underestimate the challenge. If you do, such organizations will remain the exception rather than the rule—for most people, a mere dream.

Originally published in May 2013. Reprint R1305H

TERESA M. AMABILE is the Edsel Ford Bryant Professor of Business Administration at Harvard Business School and a coauthor of *The Progress Principle: Using Small Wins to Ignite Joy, Engagement, and Creativity at Work* (Harvard Business Review Press, 2011).

MARCUS BUCKINGHAM is the head of people and performance research at the ADP Research Institute. He is coauthor of *Nine Lies About Work: A Freethinking Leader's Guide to the Real World* (Harvard Business Review Press, 2019).

ROBIN J. ELY is the Diane Doerge Wilson Professor of Business Administration at Harvard Business School and the faculty chair of the HBS Gender Initiative.

HEIDI K. GARDNER is a distinguished fellow at the Center on the Legal Profession and faculty chair of the Accelerated Leadership Program at Harvard Law School. She is the author of *Smart Collaboration: How Professionals and Their Firms Succeed by Breaking Down Silos* (Harvard Business Review Press, 2017).

FRANCESCA GINO is a behavioral scientist and the Tandon Family Professor of Business Administration at Harvard Business School. She is the author of the books *Rebel Talent: Why It Pays to Break the Rules at Work and in Life* and *Sidetracked: Why Our Decisions Get Derailed, and How We Can Stick to the Plan* (Harvard Business Review Press, 2013). Follow her on Twitter @francescagino.

ROB GOFFEE is an emeritus professor of organizational behavior at the London Business School. He is a coauthor of *Why Should Anyone Be Led By You?*, *Clever*, and *Why Should Anyone Work Here?* (all published by Harvard Business Review Press).

ASHLEY GOODALL is the senior vice president of leadership and team intelligence at Cisco Systems. He is coauthor of *Nine Lies About Work: A Freethinking Leader's Guide to the Real World* (Harvard Business Review Press, 2019).

LINDA A. HILL is the Wallace Brett Donham Professor of Business Administration at Harvard Business School. She is the author of *Becoming a Manager* and coauthor of *Being the Boss* and *Collective Genius* (all published by Harvard Business Review Press).

GARETH JONES is a visiting professor at the IE Business School in Madrid. He is coauthor of *Why Should Anyone Be Led By You?*, *Clever*, and *Why Should Anyone Work Here?* (all published by Harvard Business Review Press).

STEVEN J. KRAMER is an independent researcher, writer, and consultant. He is a coauthor of *The Progress Principle: Using Small Wins to Ignite Joy, Engagement, and Creativity at Work* (Harvard Business Review Press, 2011).

KENT LINEBACK spent many years as a manager and an executive in business and government. He is a coauthor of *Collective Genius: The Art and Practice of Leading Innovation* (Harvard Business Review Press, 2014).

PATTY McCORD was the chief talent officer at Netflix from 1998 to 2012 and now advises startups and entrepreneurs. She is the author of *Powerful: Building a Culture of Freedom and Responsibility*.

MARK MORTENSEN is an associate professor and the chair of the Organizational Behaviour Area at INSEAD. He researches, teaches, and consults on issues of collaboration, organizational design and new ways of working, and leadership.

TSEDAL NEELEY is an associate professor at Harvard Business School and the founder of the consulting firm Global Matters. She is the author of *The Language of Global Success: How a Common Tongue Transforms Multinational Organizations*. Follow her on Twitter @tsedal.

CHRISTINE PEARSON is a professor of global leadership at Thunderbird School of Global Management.

CHRISTINE PORATH is a professor of management at Georgetown University and the author of *Mastering Civility: A Manifesto for the Workplace*.

CATHERINE H. TINSLEY is the Raffini Family Professor of Management at Georgetown University's McDonough School of Business and the faculty director of the Georgetown University Women's Leadership Institute.

MICHAEL D. WATKINS is a cofounder of Genesis Advisers, a professor at IMD Business School, and the author of *The First 90 Days* and *Master Your Next Move* (both published by Harvard Business Review Press).

Index